The 9 Principles of Self-Healing

GW00692217

A FULL CIRCLE BOOK

The 9 Principles of Self-Healing

The 40 Day Program to Absolute Wellness

How to turn any healing crisis into
an opportunity to wake up and be free

by

Paula Horan

&

Narayan Chöyin Dorje

FULL
CIRCLE

THE 9 PRINCIPLES OF SELF-HEALING
© Paula Horan & Narayan Choyin Dorje

First Indian Paperback Edition, 2001
First Reprint, February 2003
Second Reprint, May 2003
Third Reprint, June 2005
ISBN 81-7621-076-5

Published by FULL CIRCLE *PUBLISHING*
J-40, Jorbagh Lane, New Delhi-110003
Tel: 24620063, 55654197-98 Fax: 24645795
e-mail: fullcircle@vsnl.com

Typesetting : SCANSET

J-40, Jorbagh Lane, New Delhi-110003
Tel: 24620063, 55654197-98 Fax: 24645795

Printed at Nice Printing Press, Delhi-110051

PRINTED IN INDIA
01/05/04/06/11/SCANSET/SAP/NPP/MBB

To Papaji

V

*Who Continues to Elicit
Direct Recognition*

&

*To Each and Every One of
Our Vajrayana Teachers*

*With Wisdom and Compassion
They See to It
That the Fruit of the Path Can Be Savored
by All Beings*

Disclaimer

This book presents information and techniques that have been in use in different forms for many generations. The practices utilize a natural system inherent in the body/mind. However, the authors make no claim for effectiveness. The information offered is based on many years of combined experience, and is to be used by the reader at his or her own discretion. Because people's lives vary in circumstance, and unfold with different stages of inner growth, the same rules do not apply for everyone. In case of doubt, you are cautioned to seek professional advice, especially in relation to any symptoms that may require diagnosis or medical attention. The opinions of the authors on certain medical treatments are derived from their own experience and are in no way meant as medical advice to the readers of this book. The authors, Samaya Sattva Foundation, and the publisher of this book are not responsible in any manner, for any injury that might occur through following the instructions presented in this book.

Contents ⤾

Praise for
Paula Horan & her books

As a psychologist, Reiki Master, author and seminar leader whose warmth and inspirational teaching help motivate her students to manifest the beauty as an expression of Being itself, Paula Horan's healing has cured many people in a large number of countries. However, Paula asserts, "I do not heal anyone. People have got healed. All healing is due to pure grace".

— **The Hindu**

A spiritual connection is what reiki master Paula Horan has with India. She is as much a 'free spirit' as is humanly possible. She doesn't live or belong anywhere and passionately spreads "the loving message of Reiki" which increases vibratory frequencies to heal the mind and body and equip it to explore higher spiritual planes.

— **The Economic Times**

There is much she offers by way of advice, guidance and pathways...

— **The Hindustan Times**

Acknowledgements

We are grateful for the opportunity to participate in this mystery, called Life, and for the privilege to share some of its precious facets through our books and seminars. We acknowledge the Grace which has touched us with what cannot be described in words, yet which enables our words to be meaningful and touch others. We wish to extend our heartfelt thanks to the trees that gave their life for the paper and for the hemp which await its turn to be used in the printing of these pages, to the water that has spread the ink and to the Earth, the elements, the sun, moon and the stars, which all made it possible for the trees to grow. There is not one thing in this vast universe that did not contribute to the realization of our endeavor, and thus we are grateful to all of the visible and invisible forces, which continue to support us with their inestimable life and life force.

Our gratitude also reaches out to all the human beings who were essential for the writing and making of this book. First, the foremost among those are our teachers who through their kindness continue to open the treasure chest of wisdom and compassion. We wish to thank our publisher for his continuing support, and our many friends in India and elsewhere for their continuing hospitality and availability in times of need. We thank Narayan's mother who gifted us with a new iBook although the old power book was still working just fine. To all the loving beings who have supported us on our path throughout time, we are in deep gratitude. May they always have happiness and the causes of happiness. May they also rest in equanimity, free from attachment and aversion.

Introduction
Healing through Wholeness

If we examine ourselves every day with mindful-ness and mental alertness, checking our thoughts, motivations, and their manifestation in external behavior, a possibility for change... can open within us. Personally, I find this very helpful in my own life.

— H.H. Dalai Lama XIV

The *9 Principles of Self-Healing* enable you to engage in deep self-inquiry and examine your life with love, compassion and unbiased understanding. The princi-ples are an invitation to get to know yourself better and to fully feel, what it really means to be human. Although in and by themselves they propose no across-the-board solution for everyone, they provide for you as an individual, the necessary tools to discover the solution that is appropriate for you.

There comes a moment in every life for re-evalua-tion, when you start to look for clarification about your own priorities and seek to determine what your next step should be. Often such times are tied in with a crisis in your state of health or well-being, or they are pro-voked through a lingering sense of dissatisfaction or disenchantment. Whatever the surface cause may appear to be, they represent a healing crisis, an opportunity to break the mold that has become too narrow for the expression of your energies. Challenging times of physical illness or emotional stuckness give you a chance to grow into a larger and more wholesome way of life. They may even afford you the rare opportunity to get to find out who you truly are, and why you are here.

If a healing crisis happens in your life, it is beneficial to welcome it wholeheartedly, even though it might pose a challenge, and even if it is in the form of an illness. Whatever happens to you, no matter how challenging, it is a message on your life's path, which if you heed, will return you to the freedom, openness, and balance that is your own true nature.

Very often, when we are struck by illness, or are depressed and disillusioned, our friends and loved-ones come with advice as to how to get rid of the problem. Or we go to see a doctor, with the result that a medication is prescribed or a procedure recommended that is supposed to make us well again. In certain cases medical treatment may be called for and even unavoidable. However, in many instances our highest priority is really to listen to ourselves and to feel our own feelings. We don't need the type of "cure" that only covers up the underlying problem and thus buries the root cause. It behooves us to first feel what is really bothering us, and with this understanding, take the action we need for the best results. We need to explore the message hidden in our discomfort or discontent and discover the lesson we are here to learn.

The 9-Principles of Self-Healing fulfill this substantial need, for a tool that can address times of crisis or general bewilderment. Much like all natural remedies, the principles are not a cure-all in the sense that they necessarily give instant relief. With your participation, however, they can be a great help for you in uncovering the best possible remedies to the challenges that you are facing. The book, therefore, is about mindfulness and the attitude with which to cultivate it. It is designed to help you discover a wholesome attitude that will contribute to a basic and all pervading sense of health and well-being. The approach contained on these pages can work wonders, if you follow it with dedication and consistency. The book sets a certain tone. It suggests a path. When you follow it and fully apply yourself, you will grow through your own experience. You will learn to trust yourself. You will begin to appreciate your intuition. You will discover a new dimension to the intelligence, which resides within your own Heart. Slowly and gradually, you will experience an increased sense of understanding, balance and a quiet, unassuming self-confidence. To help you access these and other life affirming qualities is the purpose of this book.

The 9 Principles of Self-Healing are meant to support and inspire you in rediscovering your own innate ability to heal. The principles will help you learn to appreciate yourself and your life in a deeply loving and caring manner, without taking your impermanent "self" too seriously. You will begin to see that healing happens through recognizing the vastness and the mystery that you truly are – a vastness, which speaks even through your very ordinary and mundane experiences and feelings.

In Master Hua-Ching Ni's translation of the timeless Chinese classic, the *I Ching*, or *Book of Changes*, we find a pertinent passage of his own comments to the text where he quotes his father. It beautifully illustrates our purpose, as he states: "There is no incurable disease. There are only incurable people". Which infers that to heal we have to take responsibility for our own life and health, with the attitude of loving kindness and self-respect. Ultimately, we all have to live out the life that we have molded. If we take on the role of the "victim" and then unconsciously expect others to play the "rescuer", can any lasting benefit be achieved? Can there be good health and a basic sense of well-being, if we choose to remain unconscious of most of what is happening to us day in and day out? Can someone else really save us from ourselves?

Today, there are a lot of discussions about a necessary shift in paradigm. Much has been written about a pending transformation from a mechanical and machine oriented one, to a holistic approach in health care. Yes, such a shift would make things easier and more wholesome for the healing profession as well as for the patients, by simply re-introducing the human factor. What is exciting though, is that we can all complete this shift here and now. We don't have to wait for outside phenomena to happen, or for the general populace to become enlightened. If we wait for everyone to come around, we may very well have to wait until "kingdom come".

What is so empowering and refreshing, is that this necessary paradigm shift comes down to a simple shift in our own personal approach to life, health and happiness. Once we understand that we are the wholeness in which everything is contained, we can live our entire life from this much more spacious sense of being. Again, wholeness is not something to be realized out there. Wholeness manifests in each of our own sensations, feelings and everyday experiences. In fact there is nothing but wholeness. When we begin to examine our own life along the lines of the 40-Day Program suggested in this book, we will discover this through direct experience. When we dive into our own sensations and feelings and explore them from the inside, we begin to experience how much vaster they are than they appear to be at first glance, as mere thoughts and ideas of the mind.

The Buddha once stated that, "in this 6-foot body the entire universe is contained". This was not a concept or a lofty idea for him, but a reality. He spoke from experience. It is the type of experience this book intends to introduce its readers to, even if as a mere glimpse. When followed with the right attitude, even glimpses can be transforming, no matter how vague and ill defined they are. Glimpses can sometimes save a life. Intuition when heeded, can lead to liberating action. Just pause and reflect on this phrase for a moment: *"In this 6-foot body the entire universe is contained."* What a powerful message! How uplifting as a hypothesis! How awesomely liberating as an experience! If the Buddha is right and not just speaking metaphorically (and he isn't!), there are indeed majestic abilities to create balance and self-healing that lie dormant in us. No less than the powers inherent in the entire cosmos, as a matter of fact.

As you participate in the program you will discover that you can also access them in a very simple manner: through whatever circumstance manifests in your life. Every cell of the body accommodates all of the memory capacity and all of the information, contained in the entire body/mind. Every emotional or sensory experience we have can serve as a gateway, to access all the other emotional or sensory experiences, we have had in the so-called "past". We are not cut off from the knowledge of all of our lifetimes.

Everything is right here, and everything is accessible, if we choose to notice. The choice we have available to us time and again, is between awareness and simply slipping back into unconsciousness. The more we choose awareness, the healthier we become, and also happier, until even these concerns fade in the background and get lost in the pure appreciation of whatever appears, independent of its emotional charge.

The 9 Principles of Self-Healing map out a path to wellness entirely accessible to everyone whose heart and mind are open enough to work with them. Although they evoke our spiritual nature, they are also very simple and practical, and don't require secret teachings or any knowledge of esoteric lore. They do not claim to heal you from every ailment, but when you apply them in your life, they can very well guide you to awaken your own inner intelligence to the cure that you need.

If you wish to utilize the program and stay in touch with other participants, you can contact them through the web-site, which is given at the end of the book. You can also find inspiration and exchange experiences through an off-line chat room. If you wish to set up a support group to study and apply the 40-Day Program together with others, chapter 12 gives further suggestions. If you also wish to share your observations and experiences with us, let us know what's happening, through our web-site.

It is our sincere conviction that the more people really feel, know, and understand themselves, thereby becoming healthier, happier and more balanced, the more the Earth will also become balanced. This in turn will evoke a healthier life for all concerned. If you have felt drawn to purchase this book, it may be a sign that the time has come for you, to examine your life and open up and receive the full and incredible gift that you have been carrying all along – in the depth of your feelings, and ultimately in the depth of your Heart.

Paula Horan
Narayan Chöyin Dorje

Jnanasagara Dvipa, December 6th, 2000

The Purpose of the 9 Principles

Does this path have a heart?
If it does, the path is good.
If it doesn't, the path is of no use.

— **Carlos Castenada.**

The *9 Principles of Self-Healing* are only nine of the countless facets of the Diamond of Consciousness. They help us to better understand how imbalances and ailments arise, how they effect us, and how we can soften their impact, possibly to the point of complete dissolution. They have been selected here, to facilitate our inquiry.

Furthermore, there is no hierarchical order to them, beginning with self-respect and ending with enlightenment. They are of equal value and of equal importance, as they are only representations of the greater Truth of the Consciousness that we are. They are different mirrors, set at different angles that reflect different facets of our own nature, bringing them to the fore so that they can be integrated. The idea of a hierarchy is foreign to the process of self-inquiry, and also foreign to our true nature. Hierarchies are always based on the relative values of the world and are thus impermanent. They can never reflect the totality of Consciousness.

Although there is no hierarchy to the importance of the principles, they are placed in the order in which they correspond to the themes in the nine chapters. Later, the same nine themes become steps in the 40-Day program in a way that they build on the inner progress that is initiated by your work with the previous theme. In this way, there is a certain practical order in their presentation. The completion of each step leads successively to the ability to complete the one that follows.

A good way to work with these nine principles, is to first read them slowly one at a time, perhaps only one a day, followed by the accompanying chapter and then reflect on them. They are a good and very concise introduction to what is presented in each of the chapters which follow. They can also serve as a good lead into the actual 40-Day Program. They are written in evocative prose so that they will resonate in you. Therefore don't think about them so much as objects of your inquiry, but as mirrors. Give them the chance to refract what you wish to discover in yourself. They are also listed additionally for easy reference after chapter 12.

1

The Principle of Self Respect

When we have self respect, we don't tolerate
being rushed. Even when under pressure we
manage to remain deliberate. We savor each
moment and come to our own conclusions when
and how it feels right for us. We honor the
world by truly perceiving it. We honor ourselves
by allowing the space and time we need, in all
of our endeavors. In this way, every moment of
our life is an invitation for self-discovery and an
opportunity for the recognition of Truth.

Chapter 1

Slow Down!

The most important point concerns ignorance, for the entities and causes for all illness derive from ignorance. From ignorance there is obscurations due to which we do not recognize unsalutary states of mind as faulty...
— Dr. Yeshe Donden

The first step toward self-healing of either emotional imbalances or physical ailments is to slow down. As we slow down, we have a chance to perceive what is really happening in our lives. We can then better observe and understand our inner state of being and its mirror, our outer situation in life. Such understanding affords us the opportunity to take responsibility and initiate the actions necessary to alter whatever is bothering us.

Illness most often arises when we are too busy or overwrought to pay attention to the signals that point to where our true priorities lie. The causal factors of a common cold are a case in point. The two main reasons for "catching" a cold are:

• You are carrying a lot of grief or anger and have suppressed your need to cry, and;

• You have submitted your body to too much stress, a deluge of toxins such as: air pollutants, alcohol, drugs (including unnecessary over–the–counter and prescription drugs), too much or unhealthy food.

All of these in concert with excess stress and/or lack of rest all exhaust the immune system, which now needs to purge itself.

When you slow down your pace, all of a sudden it becomes possible to feel your feelings again; the very ones you were ignoring in the first place. The neurotically busy pace of today's life-style is designed to keep you asleep to your genuine feelings. When you can barely keep your head above water just to keep up, you will fail to notice what is really going on. When you are speeding along like a rat on a wheel, there is no time to reflect and feel.

To experience emotional balance and/or health, an important step is to regain your awareness to your deepest inner feelings, your own private sense of inner knowing. True knowledge is felt, experienced – *not understood with the mind.*

You can only connect with this innate awareness when you slow down. When you slow down, you begin to get the first inkling of peace and that is the silent power, which resides within you all of the time. In ordinary circumstances, we simply do not notice, neither our innate peace nor our own power, because we are never fully present, feeling what is happening *now.* Instead we are always reminiscing or futurizing in the mind. When your mind is incessantly engaged in memory, either planning or worrying (both sure signs that you are in memory mode), you are bound to suffer. You are suffering, as you are not noticing what is the *only existing* reality - the eternal moment *now*.

Peace, balance, harmony and health exist only in your awareness of the present moment. Therefore, to notice these qualities, your attention needs to be focused, enabling you to directly experience what presents itself *now*. However, you can only perceive and be fully present, when your mind is in slow motion taking in everything consciously, rather than in the hypnotizing fast track of future projection, which is nothing but a product concocted from past memory. For example, when you take a moment to reflect, you will observe that all the great plans you have made for the future, are without exception based on what you know from the past. Thus, again, all "futurizing" only comes out of memory, out of the past that is *not* now.

This is not to say you should not make plans for the future. It is fine to let the mind plan, and experience your life, as the body takes action to fulfill the plan. The secret to happiness is to participate fully in your life, but simultaneously notice that it is all just happening, regardless of your incorrect view of yourself as a separate "doer", in other words, you as an illusory separate entity.

All body/minds play out their roles on automatic mode, much like actors in a well rehearsed role. To understand this better, it helps to explore who you actually are, which is Consciousness playing with itself as a myriad of forms. Each body/mind has no real substance as has been demonstrated by quantum physics. It is merely a dream within Consciousness that seems to have a past, present, and future.

Time (past, present, and future) and space (as a container of things), seem to be real because of the five senses of the body. Everything seems to occur, one after the other, in a linear fashion. In truth, reality is more like the dream states you experience at night, which just appear out of nowhere. While you are totally identified with the dream, you naturally assume that each character has a past history of where they came from until that moment in the dream and where they most likely will end up. The dream seems so real, but then it all just disappears when you wake up: the story, the characters all vanish much like everything in our world does at a much slower pace. Eventually everything, even planets and star systems, disappear.

The only reality is ever-present awareness – it is the only quality that exists always and doesn't change or disappear. It is who you truly are in every moment. As Consciousness, you dream up your body/ mind and play out its role like an actor in a play. The trouble is, you continually forget that it is all a play, your own creation, and so you suffer over all the dream "realities", that you as Consciousness have become identified with. The moment you drop your identification with the play by feeling what is so in the present, suffering disappears. You may even experience pain in the dream body, but you no longer suffer over the suffering.

This is what Jesus suggested when he said, "Be in the world but not of it". Simply be fully in the present moment, enjoying whatever life brings. Your only real choice in life is the attitude with which you receive or react to the circumstances that arise as part of the dream. When we slow down, we can begin to perceive the movie-like quality of reality and take a lot more in. Our perceptions become heightened and we just know intuitively how to react in every situation.

In western society, the ability to feel has been trained out of us with our short attention spans brought on by fifty years of watching too much television. Our instincts have become dulled, and it is difficult for most to tune in with the superior intelligence of Heart. In the west, and now in more parts of the world, mind rules supreme.

Most of the time, we are totally unconscious, mesmerized by the TV screen in our own mind that incessantly flashes memories and projections. These only act to filter or water down our present, while in the process also dulling our sense of presence as well as our full energetic capability. Programmed to distract us from the vastness and strength that is our true potential, this never-ending internal boob tube continually compartmentalizes our moment to moment experience. Our identification with it and the speed with which these memory slots and projections proliferate, lead to our destruction.

As the wheels of thoughts and their reactive emotions keep on spinning faster and faster, and continue to clog us up on a cellular level, they inevitably lead to sickness, old age and death. Such speed kills. The acceleration of memories and projections running through our minds, and the fact that we are completely identified with them, literally depletes us physically until our energies are spent.

Slowing down does not infer that we have to completely change our way of life and live at a snail's pace. That would be beside the point, as well as impractical. Although you may have to slow down your pace temporarily in order to tune in with the innate calm that resides within, in actual fact your outer activities can be happening as quickly as they always have. However, *when the mind moves slowly,* allowing consciousness to absorb all of the input of the outer world, a sense of calm and clarity begins to replace an otherwise chaotic sense of reality.

Most peoples' minds tend to be on the run non-stop, even if the body is still. They are constantly racing at a pace similar to the old silent black and white movies prevalent before the "talkies" were invented. This is quite the opposite of a well grounded, stable and self-empowered individual whose life may look outwardly like the jarred, neurotic pace of an old silent film, yet whose mind inwardly is like a still pond, regardless of outer appearances.

In this stillness, Truth can be felt; the Truth that is your nature.

Truth resides in your Heart, not in your mind. When you ignore truth, the body eventually gets sick, until once again you pay attention and heed your Heart.

Most emotional imbalance and illness has its roots in unhappiness, in not following your own feelings. Only your Heart can tell you what you really need. No one else can do that for you.

One way you can slow down immediately so that you can begin to feel your feelings, is to take a few long, slow, deep breaths. When you slow your breathing down, your mind slows down. You can then begin to feel your deepest feelings – the ones hidden underneath your surface level emotions.

Emotions are energetic reactions to thoughts. They begin in your etheric or energy body, as a reaction to how you interpret (with your thoughts) your moment to moment experiences. In other words, emotions are reactions to the thoughts you formulate about the circumstances that arise in your life, and they are all automatically activated and beyond your control. Due to your prior conditioning, your thoughts manifest and proliferate as a law onto themselves. Thus, there is not a thing that you can do about your emotions, which, again, are simply a reaction to your conditioned thoughts. They will come and go as they please. Forget "controlling" them, as this is a sure way for them to control you. If you try to control something, this shows you are in resistance to it, and it will only persist.

The only chance you have to let go of your emotions, is to slow down, and to notice and feel them. What you will discover is that whatever you put your full attention on simply disappears. Yet, again, you can't try and notice something in order to make it go away. If you attempt to notice something with the intention to make it go away, it will doggedly persist.

Below all surface level activity, is your own deep inner knowing that can only be directly experienced. It is the Truth you *feel* in every moment. It is where your true Peace lies, if only you will learn to listen to it.

So take a few deep breaths now before you continue reading, and notice if you begin to feel now what these words are conveying. Notice any nuances of unacknowledged feelings, especially in any dissatisfaction you are carrying.

2

The Principle of Awareness

When in harmony with the natural flow of
awareness, we notice every major and minor
aspect in the complex tapestry of our existence.
We drop the fetters of unconscious behavior
and slowly disengage from ignorance. We enter
the path of a true human being. With every
instance of conscious awareness, we water the
roots of the tree of Life and grow in Freedom.

Chapter 2

Notice What You Resist

For it is important that awake people be awake,
Or a breaking line may discourage them back
to sleep;
The signals we give – yes or no, or may be –
Should be clear: the darkness around us is deep.

- William Stafford

The second step toward self-healing of either emotional imbalances or physical ailments is to notice what we have been and are still resisting in our lives. When we adopt a willingness to notice our denial, even if it has been unconscious, by virtue of simply acknowledging it, it begins to be released. When we finally acknowledge our previously hidden resistance, we also assume a much better position to understand what keeps us stuck in emotional misery or physical discomfort in the first place. We gain direct access to the psychosomatic and karmic causes of our discomfort or illness. Such understanding affords us the opportunity to take responsibility and later explore these causes more deeply by directly feeling into them.

We know we are out of balance when we become dissatisfied. This dissatisfaction when not addressed turns into either physical illness or depression. Dissatisfaction is a wake-up call and should be heeded as the gift that it is, because it tells us immediately that we are not following our Heart.

I have seen time and again in my own body as well as in the people that I have treated over the years that illness is a temperature gauge of sorts, which shows us where our individual consciousness is out of synchronization with reality. In other words, illness is a direct reflection of certain thought forms stored in the body that we are in resistance to.

For example, years ago (from age 13-27) I was a grand mal epileptic. When I received a rebirthing (a highly effective process for emotional release) years later, I re-experienced my previous lifetime, where I had lived through the atom bomb in Hiroshima. After August 6th 1945, I remained alive in excruciating pain for three months and my mind stream carried the shock of that experience into the present incarnation. At puberty in this lifetime, due to hormonal changes or other karmic conditions, certain thought or memory crystals of the Hiroshima experience were released. From then on, whenever stress built up in my current life, I would literally spasm out a full load of withheld feelings in the form of a seizure. Somehow by age 27, the processing was complete and the epilepsy disappeared.

The karma or causal factor from an action in a past life was complete. In other words, the intense grief, rage, anger, and pain I had not processed before my death, carried over into this life and manifested as a physical disability, which literally forced me to throw off withheld feelings. As I learned to directly address my feelings in this lifetime, the epilepsy disappeared.

At age 19, I developed a tumor in my right breast, which was clearly a reaction to the sudden shocking death of my brother. The grief over his death literally got stuck in my chest (as it was a heart related issue), until I could release it. Several years later after the "death" of a seven-year relationship, I developed another tumor in the left breast – another reaction to withheld feelings in the heart.

In both cases some sort of emotional reaction was resisted and ended up manifesting in a physical form. Illness always starts in the mind. We even fall prey to accidents in the same way. Each action (karma) from previous lifetimes or from the past in this lifetime, attracts to us certain events. We all have both "good" and "bad" karma. Although there truly is no such thing as "good" or "bad", the circumstances that seem "bad" to us are simply rehashes of previous situations we have resisted.

In the two examples above, I resisted the full expression of my grief and anger. Due to this unconscious resistance, which is nothing more than a natural human tendency to avoid discomfort, those same emotions got stuck and crystallized on a physical level.

Everything is energy, including our thoughts, our emotional reaction to our thoughts, as well as our capacity to feel the ground of our Being – our intrinsic awareness.

Whenever we resist either a thought or an emotion we are resisting energy that has to go somewhere. When we can develop the ability to accept what is so in our lives in every moment, so that the energy of each particular experience can simply pass through, discomfort becomes a very temporary experience.

When experiences are acknowledged and felt fully in the moment, they occur without resistance; they do not remain or become crystallized to attract similar experiences later.

However, it is our habitual tendency to automatically resist "negative" or dense energy thoughts and emotions, such as grief, anger, rage, sadness, ambivalence and hate, which causes them to energetically congeal and get stuck in the mind-stream, and thus the body/mind. And they always get stuck and cause disease in the area of the body where that particular type of thought or emotion is typically felt.

For example, resisted "heart" feelings such as jealousy, rejected love, withheld rage and so forth, tend to crystallize in the heart area. Emotions and judgments dealing with control and power issues crystallize in the solar plexus area. Emotional pain due to sexual hurt, neglect and abuse that is not allowed to be felt and released, can easily cause uterine problems, ovarian tumors or functional impotence.

Therefore, a crucial step to releasing these congealed thoughts and judgments is to notice what you are resisting. It requires real honesty with oneself. So often we allow others, especially our close relatives, such as our parents who really mean well, to make significant life decisions for us, which may not actually suit us at all. At other times, we ourselves make incorrect decisions with disastrous results, yet are afraid later to admit the mistake and disengage ourselves from a certain course of action or path, especially if we fear we will hurt others in the process.

We often fall prey to a false sense of guilt, forgetting that although we may need to temporarily (albeit deeply) hurt another in order to change an unsuitable situation, we will eventually hurt them anyway. Unsuitable situations have the tendency to be untenable in the long run.

The bottom line is, if we do not make and follow the choices of our own innermost Heart, we will never be happy. If we are not happy, the people around us will know it because they will feel it, no matter what facade we are projecting outwardly. In the long run, they will have to suffer our unhappiness by association, for example through an illness that we accrue to help us process our self-denial. Withholding the truth from them thus also cheats them out of an opportunity to be genuinely happy.

Emotional illness or depression is so often caused by this very same denial of one's own inner needs. Depression so common in today's world, is a sign that dissatisfaction has been present for a long time – but was ignored all along.

Depression is not a feeling. It is only a *symptom of the repression of feelings* we have held in. It is a sure sign that we have been ignoring our deepest heartfelt feelings, and that we have been going along with society's dictates instead of heeding our own inner knowing. When we feel depressed or dissatisfied, with further self-examination we will discover that somehow we are resisting our own inner truth.

Whenever people come to me with life threatening illnesses, like cancer or severe suicidal depression and ask for advice, besides referring them to doctors and psychologists that I trust, I always suggest that they do some intense emotional release work. I usually recommend some deep tissue bodywork, rebirthing,

Bioenergetics, gestalt therapy or Osho's "Dynamic Meditation". I also inquire as to their general life situation, their career, and how they are relating to others both at home and on the job. If you do this with yourself, you may discover what to others might already have been obvious, but with your blinders of denial on, you may have failed to notice.

Occasionally, illnesses appear that even after extensive self-observation seem to have no rhyme or reason, at least in regard to the recent past. There is a story about the Buddha, which best illustrates this particular type of malady and elicits the best understanding of its cause: One fine day, the Buddha was sitting on the banks of a stream with one of his disciples. It was a scorching summer day, and after a few minutes the disciple noticed that the Buddha was clutching his head as if in terrible pain. He asked his Master, if he had a headache. "Yes,", the Buddha replied, "about 450 lifetimes ago I was sitting on the banks of a similar stream at about the same time of the year. It was very hot and the stream had almost completely dried up. A fish was flopping desperately in what had now become a mere puddle. I took a rock and threw it at its head to put it out of its misery. Yet I missed the spot that would have killed it instantly. Through my clumsiness I made the fish suffer even more, and I am feeling that now."

In other words, like the Buddha in the above example, sometimes illness or mishaps befall us from some long forgotten karma. It is important to grasp, however, that although at the highest order of understanding we do not actually have karma, because in essence we are not the body, and not the mind. In truth we are Consciousness that dreams the body/mind. Nevertheless, we as Consciousness or Buddha Mind still have to put up with the karma of the body/mind. Our body/mind through its mind stream, is connected to many other body/minds of related previous incarnations, in all the different linked past lifetimes.

Whenever we have hurt another or ourselves (for hurting another is essentially not different from hurting oneself), the hurt of this action attracts to us a situation so that we experience directly the results of these past actions. The trick is, we will never know and thus often least expect when these long forgotten actions will bear fruit. As my own Master Papaji used to say: "When the circumstances for vasanas arise, the vasanas arise." Vasanas, of course, are ingrained patterns due to karma or past actions.

In the above story, Buddha found himself in an environment and circumstance similar to one from a previous incarnation. The previous cause (his throwing of the stone) finally found the right circumstance for the effect to manifest, and thus complete the cycle. The difference in the result or effect on Buddha, however, is that although Buddha experienced the pain of the headache, he did *not suffer* over it – because he did not identify with it and thus *not resist* it.

Pain, whether emotional or physical becomes worse and turns into real suffering when we resist it. If instead we direct all of our attention to it and actually imagine it expanding (fully allowing it to be there and not trying to make it go away), it begins to dissipate. Often the memory of the cause will even arise when we adopt an attitude of exploring inner space and can thus observe our discomfort without resistance, without trying to make it go away. Simply feeling it in its entirety is, again, the most important thing.

Yet, before we can really feel it, we must be able to direct our attention to what we resist. We must become aware of any concealed blockages or screens that deflect our awareness from our heart. We can do this by honestly taking stock and acknowledge all the things that we resent in our lives. Feeling that resistance fully, is then the next logical step.

3

The Principle of Letting Go

By finally diving into our feelings and exploring them from the inside out, we let go of unhealthy clinging. The power that our unconscious and unacknowledged feelings once had over us, from this moment onward flows through us. The congealed power that kept us stuck and in bondage is now liberated to fuel our creativity. Feeling our feelings fully and letting them go of their own accord, we increase our awareness of the hidden beauty within all appearances. As we embrace our feelings, we are rejuvenated, becoming more flexible and responsive.

Chapter 3

Feel What You Resist

The wise discriminate between
The Real and the unreal.
They know what is Real and so allow
Their feelings and thoughts to arise
Because they know all is One and the same!
In this way there is no attachment
And no suffering.

- Papaji

Once you have examined what it is you are resisting, the next step is to feel your resistance to it. Ruminating about resistance mentally will never free you of its effect. Neither will any attempt to make it go away. The paradox is that to release resistance, you have to first acknowledge it fully, allowing it to be there. Then, with the attitude of an adventurer exploring inner space, you just dive right in. Ultimately, to release resistance, you have to feel it.

To feel something does not necessarily mean that you have to become emotional about it, although very often emotions will arise in the process. To feel, in this context, means to direct your awareness to an object or idea from the perspective of your *heart*, rather than your head. It means to notice consciously *with feeling* how a particular idea or thought effects your entire body/mind.

For example, if you have come to the conclusion that your illness, dissatisfaction or depression is the result of an unhappy relationship, then you first need to acknowledge your resistance to the relationship as it is. If you have failed to express your dissatisfaction to your partner, feel your resistance to doing so. Imagine yourself beginning a conversation with this person, and all of the resistance this image brings up.

Put all your attention on your resistance to asking for what you need. Feel how feeling this resistance manifests in your body. Feel, if there is tension in your face, in your chest, in your back, or in your belly. Place your hands on your heart and let it speak what so far has been unspoken. Feel your yearning as you speak it. Feel your need, and imagine the energy of that need expanding. Feel it growing bigger, expanding in every direction all around you. Keep focusing on it for however long it takes, until it seems there is nothing more to be expanded.

If you are yearning for some sort of shift in your life. If you have gone against your own grain. If you have denied your own heartfelt desire out of a sense of guilt or obligation to others – feel that now. Feel your resistance to fulfilling your desire, and expand that feeling of resistance in every direction, in every dimension in which it exists. It is important to remember that every thought, such as resistance, just like any physical sensation, is simply a specific energy frequency. As you direct your attention to any mental resistance, or to the physical sensations, which manifest in reaction to it, your very attention acts like a focused laser beam that then begins to dissipate whatever it is focused on. Just like laser surgery can burn away kidney stones and clogged arteries, the laser of your heartfelt attention on whatever ails you, does the same trick.

There is only one "catch-22". When you are dealing with resistance, you cannot direct your attention to it with the idea of making it go away. For as we all know, whatever we resist, persists. So if you direct your attention to anything (especially resistance) with the motivation to make it go away, this itself is resistance, and it will consequently not dissipate. Trying to make resistance go away will simply not work.

Whenever you want to make something go away, this points to the fact that you are attached to it in a negative way; you are *identified* with it. Whatever you are attached to in either a positive or negative way will not disappear. The important thing to notice, once again, is that you are *identified with the resistance*.

In laser surgery, the laser couldn't care less whether the kidney stone goes away or not. The laser's purpose is only to beam out its penetrating light. Whatever it is directed at, it couldn't care less. Thus it doesn't have to struggle to make the kidney stone or the clogged artery disappear. In the same way, if you direct your heart motivated attention on any idea or emotion with the *simple intention to explore* whatever it evokes, then what you focus on will simply disappear. In effect, it will evaporate in the laser beam of Consciousness – as long as you are *not* resisting it. As long as you are not trying to make something go away.

This is so difficult for human beings to *grasp*, but it *is* the key to the equanimity of a Buddha. A Buddha is neither attached nor detached. He or she simply *is*. In other words, even when a Buddha appears to be attached, he or she is simultaneously detached. The opposite is equally true. Boggles the mind? Yes, it does because only your Heart can understand this. Because once again, this reality can only be felt.

It is simply a habit of the *mind*, caught in duality, to resist uncomfortable thoughts or feelings, which then only makes them stick. A simple way to change this habit, is to develop a sense of wonderment to whatever arises in every moment, in every circumstance, whether it is happy or sad, good or bad, comfortable or uncomfortable. This is why Jesus said it is important to "be as a child". A young child, still unconditioned by its parents and society's programming, is always in wonderment.

In truth, the only difference between an average human being and a fully Awakened and Enlightened one, is that the average person is literally constipated on a cellular level with all of their beliefs and judgments, which falsely justify an illusory separate self. All of our conditioning that keeps us small, believing that we are "not good enough", that we are "unworthy", also keeps us on a constant merry-go-round of approval seeking. We fall prey to going against our own heartfelt wishes in order to buy love or approval from others, and this literally makes us sick. We fail to notice that the real love we seek has been inside of us all along, that in reality, it is omnipresent.

Not only do we get lost in approval seeking because of this false belief in an imaginary, separate self, which seeks love from an illusory outside, we also get lost in and become controlled by a need for security. This false sense of separation from others due to our identification with the five senses of the body, makes us forget that we are not the body. The body is inside of us, inside of who we really are – and so are all other bodies! Truly there is only one Self in the universe, manifesting as myriads of countless frequencies, which through the sense of sight in its billions of vibrational forms, creates an illusory sense of many beings – to those self same forms.

The reality is that there is only one *Beingness* happening all at once, not many beings, and that is the realization of a Buddha. A Buddha identifies as THAT, which manifests all "bodies" – and remains THAT in all of its manifestations. When Jesus said, "in my father's house there are many mansions", he was speaking of this same phenomena to people who had not heard of quantum physics.

Even in this day and age, of scientific proof that there is no separation, the five senses still keep us hypnotized in the illusion of a subject/object reality. We identify with the subject, the body, and its mental protector, the ego, and forget that who we truly ARE, which is consciousness, is never born and never dies.

Because we believe we are separate, we grasp at an illusory "outside" for love and approval. Because we believe we are the body, we suffer terrible insecurity. Because we identify with these things, it becomes a terrific problem to have a body, to have thoughts, beliefs and emotions.

Once we wake up and realize that we are not the body/mind, it is then not a problem to have a body, to have feelings, to have certain thoughts, to have emotions. They all become passing phenomena, and even in their passing they are pure evocations of the stillness that we truly are – whether we are having a "good" day or a "bad" day. Living in comic circumstances or tragic circumstances. And the secret to waking up is to FEEL. We can never really *know* what is so because It is too vast to "know", but we can surely feel and experience That, which we truly Are.

All illness, all disease arises when we resist feeling something. We resist feeling particular circumstances because we are *identified* with them in a certain way. In our ignorance, we give this dream reality more credence than it deserves. We take it (and ourselves) much too seriously, and we resist whatever we don't understand. Through resistance, we literally dam up energy. This dammed-up energy has to go somewhere. Resistance starts as a thought, turns into an emotional reaction, and then gets stuck in the corresponding area in the body, depending on the type of thought.

Feel what you have been resisting that you need. Feel what you have been resisting that you don't want. Write a list of both and read them out loud from your heart. "I need... (fill in the blank)!". "I don't want... (fill in the blank)!" Read them with passion when no one is around, so that you don't feel shy about shouting them out with fervor. Finally, when you are ready, read them with equal passion to a friend or partner whom you trust.

Read them over and over and over,... until the energy is dissipated and with whatever is left, put your laser beam of attention on it and imagine it expanding. First feel your desire (or resistance in the case of what you don't want) expanding until it dissipates, and then expand the object of your desire or resistance. Remember to do this with the open attitude of exploration – like a laser beam of wonderment exploring inner space.

The key is always to allow yourself to *feel* what is so. Do not judge yourself for any feeling that arises. Simply feel it. Then expand it. Always in wonderment. Always with the intention to explore. YOU ARE the jackpot at the end of your quest. Your feelings will guide you home to your very own Heart.

As you learn to attend to the various thought forms that arise during the day with a vigilant, yet heartfelt attention, you will discover that your old conditioned patterns seem to melt away. Your "buttons" will get pushed from time to time, but in the light of vigilant attention, they lose their charge. In this way, you effectively "knock the wind out of the sails" of your old unconscious resistance. Focused heartfelt attention is naturally unconditioned. It never judges, so it evokes no resistance. With no resistance, all experiences, comfortable or uncomfortable, simply flow through Life as one never ending, continuous movie with all its ups and downs, tragedies and comedies. You, however, remain as the still silent screen on which the various dramas are projected.

With the laser beam of your awareness in full operation, you cease to be internally swayed by the illusion of "outer" events. With full participation, however, in the movie, you allow your consciousness to engage completely in all the ups and downs, fully feeling, neither attached nor detached, learning anew in the letting go, the incredible Bliss of Existence.

4

The Principle of Courage

We are conditioned to relegate what we don't
know into the shadowy recesses of the mind.
What lurks in the shadows, we usually fear. By
summoning courage we are able to face the
shadows, which are only the projections of our
fear. The greatest fear we have is that of death.
Death can be physical, as in the body dying.
Death can be symbolic, as in the ego being
exposed as the illusion it is. By facing our
greatest fear with courage, it becomes our
fiercest ally and protector, similar to the darkest
shadow that eventually reveals its innate light.

Chapter 4

Address Your Fear

Fear always distorts our perception
And confuses us as to what is going on.
All fear is past and only Love is here.

-Gerald Jampolsky

As long as we are alive and still *identified* with the body/mind, we will always crave approval and security. Once you begin to focus on and fervently pronounce your need as suggested earlier, your fear of asking for it and the fear of taking the courage to go after it, will inevitably arise. At some point your fear of losing someone's approval, or your fear of losing your security, will also arise. For the psyche to heal, these fears have to be felt and addressed.

To ever be really free, the need for security and approval must be completely dropped. The paradox is, that the way to free yourself, the way to drop this need, is to admit that you seek approval and that you need love. The way to freedom is also to admit that you need security, in every situation that it arises, because the moment you admit it, the need for security dissipates and you transcend it.

Paula can give a good example of how this works from her own life: "I truly have been blessed, in that

I have had amazing opportunities to travel, to study and to learn from some remarkable teachers. From the time I left home at 17 to my late 30s, Grace paved the way in all my endeavors - except for one, and that was in the area of my primary relationships with men. In actual fact, I attracted some wonderful men into my life, but in all cases there seemed to be some major block when it came to any real commitment. In my late 20s and early 30s I felt a strong impulse to get married and have children, but a man with the same interest never manifested. After a number of years, at one point, I had a powerful experience, which finally brought home to me the key element I had been missing all along.

When I was 35, I fell in love with an Icelander. I used to teach periodically in Reykjavik on my way back and forth between the US and Europe. We met on one of my trips when I decided to do some cross country riding, a popular way to explore Iceland. This particular man was a high school teacher as well as a superb equestrian, who guided tours on horseback during the summer months. After a brief meeting to discuss which ride I would take, we both began to have dreams about each other that seemed to take place in Mongolia. We didn't see each other for about a week, but when I met him again to begin my short riding trek, he invited me for dinner the next night. Somehow during our conversation, the extraordinary synchronicity of our dreams came up. The rest was history. What seemed like some old unfinished relationship, was rekindled that night. We began to see each other a lot and eventually decided to get married.

At that time, a family emergency called me away for a couple of months, and when I returned it seemed the flame had died out. An old girlfriend of his, who had got wind of his new relationship, re-entered the scene to lure him back. I was heart-broken. Soon thereafter I left Iceland. But a few months later, I finally had the opportunity to clear my feelings of attachment to my friend. The particular exercise I used to enhance my feelings and expand them had such a profound result, I knew beyond any shadow of a doubt that I was free, and that my love at this point was unconditional.

So I was very amazed when six months later, I kept having a strong nagging desire to go back to Iceland and see my friend. It just did not make sense. I signed up for one of his long riding tours and flew back to Reykjavik. He picked me up at the airport and proceeded to drop me off with another tour leader. In the car, I couldn't help wondering, why I'd really come. I still felt complete in his presence in regard to our previous relationship, but then I also sensed in some uncanny way that something in me was not complete. In regard to what this was, I had no clue.

As it turned out, I ended up touring with a group of Swedish women. I became friendly with one, and over a few days shared my quandary. Then on about the seventh night of the ride, I woke up and felt this incredible yearning in my heart. At first, I couldn't find words for it. I went outside into that beautiful Icelandic night, and as I stared at the star-filled sky the words began to form. "I need you", I cried. I spread my arms and cried again, "I need you". I walked a long way from the lodge and began to shout over and over again, "I need you, I need you!", until I started to cry and then sob.

Somehow, at a certain point it hit me: In all of my relationships with men over a 20 year period, I had never been able to say, "I need you". It had been easy to say, "I love you", but somehow to say, "I need you", was just too threatening. It made me feel too vulnerable. I realized that I had always been afraid of having a man try to control me. So, somehow on an unconscious level, I'd kept up the appearance of a "strong powerful Paula".

That night, I wasn't only saying "I need you" to my Icelandic lover, I was saying it to all the previous men in my life who I had never been able to fully open up to, but most of all, to my own Heart. I had finally let it speak. That night I did feel complete. And it was not long after that I did meet the man I've now been married to for several years and to whom I can easily say, "I need you".

The realization that really hit home to me on that starry Icelandic night, was the amazing paradox that, at the point I had been able to say with all my heart, "I need you", my need simply disappeared. I was free!

Another layer of this same fear was peeled off a short time later when I first met my Heart Teacher, Shri H.W.L. Poonja or Papaji (a true Jnani "one with direct knowledge" or *Buddha*, "one who has woken up"), and expressed my desire to drop my attachment to my mind. He helped me see that half of the time I was asking for help with my mind, rather than asking from my Heart. Waiting patiently with me for almost 15 minutes after he had instructed me to put my hands over my heart, and to ask only for what my heart wanted, what finally found its way to the surface was an imploring, heartfelt, "I need you."

Being an American, I have been trained to be self-reliant, which also affected my approach to spirituality. Something deep inside me knew however, that it

was time to ask for help from a mature being, someone who had direct experience of THAT which is
beyond the limitations of the conditioned human
mind. Having had my own share of deceitful gurus,
asking for help was a scary proposition.

As soon as I spoke of my need for him, Papaji asked
me specifically what I needed. The answer sprang up
naturally, "Love". Tears came to my eyes, and I laughed
and cried as I looked deeply into master's eyes. Eyes
which held no judgment, no expectations, only love.
The same eyes that over the next five years would help
release me from lifetimes of karma and, most of all, of
the vestiges of unconscious fear."

Fear is a manifestation of doubt. It is an acute lack
of trust in the universe and thus in your Self. Once we
come to understand that all the unpleasant experiences we manifest, are simply mirrors of our own past
deeds, we can shift our attitude from one of blame,
from that of a helpless victim, to a fully responsible
and fearless human being.

To experience fear when a tiger is about to pounce
on you so that you experience an appropriate adrena-
line rush and can then either fight back or run for your
life, is one thing. To spend your life in fear of paper
tigers (which is an apt description for most human
fears), is another. The secret is to cultivate a willingness
to face your fears straight on. Basically, whatever you
are resisting in your life is due to some fear.

So, if your response on day 3 of the program is, "I
don't resist anything", or "I don't need anything",
what you might now ask yourself is, "are you truly
happy?" If you are sick, either emotionally or physically, there is definitely something festering that needs

to be felt. What is it that you really want that you have been denying yourself? What have you been afraid to allow yourself to receive? Feel it. Also feel your fear of asking for it. Feel your fear of rejection. Fully. And decide to ask for it anyway.

You may not get what you ask for the first time around, but eventually you will, if you persist. You will never get what you want, however, if you don't first ask for it.

Trust yourself. Trust the universe. Once your desires have manifested enough times, you will finally learn that nothing is outside of yourself. As Buddha mind, everything is inside of you, including the entire cosmos.

Until this becomes your direct experience, however, feel your need, and feel your fear of asking for what you need. Feel your vulnerability, which is only your heart calling out and feeling what is so. It is actually what makes you so beautiful as a human being and, paradoxically, your greatest strength. Just like small children who are still open to their feelings and can sense when someone has negative vibrations and avoid them; when you allow yourself to feel from your heart, you will never be misled or waste your time with tyrants. So, allow your heart to feel your true feelings. Let it guide you to more appropriate circumstances. Allow your heart to love even the fear that you sometimes feel.

5

The Principle of Compassion

To be free is to let go of the conditioning of the past, as well as any hope for the future. As long as we can't forgive what has happened in the past we remain fettered. To forgive therefore, is a gesture of true compassion. It frees us from the bondage of past history. It severs the rope with which our grudges have tied others to our destiny, thereby releasing our burdens as well as theirs.

When unconditional, true compassion can reach out in complete openness as if with a thousand seeing hands.

Chapter 5

Let There Be Forgiveness

Guilt, as experienced in Western culture, is connected with hopelessness and discouragement, and is past-oriented. Genuine remorse, however, is a healthy state of mind – it is future-oriented, connected with hope, and causes us to act, to change.

— *H.H. Dalai Lama XIV*

One of the biggest issues we often resist unknowingly is forgiveness. Whether in regard to ourselves or another, the inability to forgive can stew in the subconscious mind and carry over for lifetimes. Not forgiving yourself or another is a way of hanging on to past memories, which keeps the same tendencies happening again and again. As human beings in the present era of mass media, we are conditioned more than ever to control and manipulate each other with guilt and obligation. Not only do we make silent unconscious agreements with each other such as "I'll put up with your masks, if you put up with mine", but we also unconsciously bully each other to tow certain social lines, even when it may be deleterious to us on a personal level.

One example is the person who is encouraged or even pushed to go into a career that fulfills a parents' desire and who acquiesces and goes against his or her own natural inclinations. Or we may unconsciously choose a spouse who turns out to have a totally different value system and who provokes us with daily circumstances, which go against our nature. Because of the commitments we make at times to what may turn out to be difficult circumstances, our obligations sometimes evolve into great burdens. Whenever we begin to feel burdened, resentment creeps in, and we begin to blame the other.

We tend to forget that it was we who made the choice to take on a certain commitment, no matter how coerced these choices may have seemed when we look at them in retrospect. The fact of the matter is that we always have a choice to leave or change our circumstances, even if the society we live in makes it seem like we can't make that choice. It is important to always remember this because, when you can remember that you are where you are, because you chose it, you take your own power back. If you blame others for your choices, you end up putting yourself in the powerless role of the victim.

Sometimes after further contemplation, you may decide you'd rather keep the obligation than go against society's grain. If you decide to stay in your present circumstance, sometimes the simple acknowledgment that it has been your choice all along, can shift things energetically in your favor – although there is no guarantee. When you make a conscious decision to be somewhere because it is your choice, your resistance to that particular circumstance disappears. The people around you feel the shift in your attitude and generally react in a positive way.

When you take full responsibility for all of the situations you find yourself in, knowing full well that all circumstances are karmic, you tend not to put out the vibrations of blame, which is the very thing that puts people off and creates static in relationships.

If you are in a situation in which you have been badly abused by another, before you can truly forgive it may be necessary to do some very deep emotional processing. Ultimately, to be free of the imprisoning energy of blame, whatever emotions are still held in, have to be fully felt. When we allow ourselves without judgment to feel through long buried memories, they begin to dissipate in the laser beam of focused loving attention. It is our openness to allowing whatever is there to be there, which invokes real healing.

To be able to feel the unconditional love, which is inherent in forgiveness, the withheld anger, rage and hatred have to go. Finding a suitable therapist to help guide you through such feelings should be high on your priority list, if you are suffering from a debilitating disease or depression. Often cancer heals rapidly when the feelings held behind it are finally processed and let go of. Depression (really only a repression of feelings) also is relieved when the feelings behind it are acknowledged. Emotional release type bodywork, rebirthing and the Osho dynamic meditation are just a few possibilities that are available to unlock withheld feelings.

The key (and the difficulty) is to find a mature therapist who has willingly processed his or her own unacknowledged feelings. Regardless of the technique that is used, a person can only guide you as deep in your own withheld feelings as they have gone with their own. The importance of addressing one's own feelings, cannot be stressed enough. To the degree that we hold onto our feelings (instead of really feeling them and letting them go through), is to the same degree that we remain unconscious, not really living our life to its full potential.

Another type of feeling that we hold onto is shame. Usually in almost everyone's life there are at least one or two incidents that we feel terribly ashamed of. Very often these are in regard to memories of sexual exper-imentation as a child or young adult,. because of the degree of sexual repression in society. Regardless of the theme, however, it is important to remember that all human beings, including yourself, always do the best that they can with the knowledge they have in the present moment.

As my Master Papaji used to say: "There is nothing to be proud of and also nothing to feel guilty or ashamed of." What this really means, is that every-thing we do when identified with the body/mind, is the result of our conditioning. The choices we seem to make are not real choices in the truest sense of the word. For example, when you look back to the time you were born, you will realize that you did not choose your parents. You did not choose your siblings, or your playmates. You did not choose the environment where you lived, or the teachers and the school that you attended. Yet, all these elements are what conditioned you into the person you are today. They determine what so-called "choices" you are now making.

You may subscribe to the new age belief that you chose your parents and therefore all the concomitant circumstances in your life. However, unless you are a very advanced bodhisattva, in actual fact, you were magnified to your circumstances in a totally unconscious way, propelled by the push and pull of karma.

In other words, virtually all the choices that human beings make, are very much unconscious. Like actors sleepwalking through a play memorized long ago, people act and react in daily circumstances totally oblivious as to who they really are. If you can begin to really observe the ignorance in which, as the separate entity you think you are, you perform virtually all of your actions, you will understand how there is truly nothing to be proud of and nothing to feel guilty about.

Noticing these things is the beginning of awareness. When we can see how faultless we really are, we can begin to feel real compassion for our state as a human being. It then becomes easy to feel compassion for ourselves as well as all others who are in the same state.

The paradox is, that real choice dawns in us, when we finally grasp that there is never really any choice. The intelligent choice, if at all, is to forgive. Truly no person in their heart of hearts wants to hurt another, including you. The horrors we call "evil" on this planet are the result of sheer ignorance. Too many misdeeds playing themselves out on top of one another. But somehow "the buck stops here". It stops with us when we choose to forgive. As we forgive ourselves and others, we fan the fire of awareness in ourselves. Others then receive it as if by osmosis.

With awareness comes the beginning of real choice. The choice to recognize who we truly are. We are not just an unconscious actor in a play. We, as Consciousness, are actually the omnipresent playwright who has dreamed this entire play with all of its infinite characters and realities.

As Consciousness, we are blameless purity devoid of pride. But as long as we doubt this, as long as we continue to fall back and solely identify as an isolated character with all its pride and guilt, forgiveness will serve as the great reminder and bring us back into the Heart of Compassion.

6

The Principle of Responsibility

This principle is also called the Principle of Empowerment, because taking on and fulfilling responsibility is the only truly empowering and satisfying experience for a human being. When we start taking responsibility, we also start to master life and cease being a victim, tossed around by circumstance. Responsibility culminates in the experience that as Consciousness, we are the Creator of our entire life. As the creator we can never be powerless victims. Once we experience this indivisible Truth, we are indeed home free.

Chapter 6

Take Action!

*Thinking and talking about the Integral Way
are not the same as practicing it.
Who ever became a good rider by talking about
horses?
If you wish to embody the Tao, stop chattering
and start practicing.*

— *Hua Hu Ching*

No matter what is troubling you, there comes a moment when you have to do something about it. It doesn't matter if it is a minor irritation, a lingering sense of dissatisfaction or a full blown ailment, like a severe illness. At some point, and in some cases very quickly, you do have to take appropriate action to meet the challenge.

However, blind action is as dangerous as total lack of action. That is why the suggestion to take action is introduced only now, after having explored ways to deal with the cause of your imbalance or ailment. A full understanding of your situation, felt and integrated from within, will be a great asset and can guide you to the right kind of action. Many people react without first feeling into their challenges and then, in the next step, try to logically analyze what can be done. They take action too fast and compound their trouble until it eventually becomes unmanageable and they are crushed by circumstances.

We had a good friend (he is deceased now) who many years ago was diagnosed during a regular check-up with full-blown cancer of both the prostate and kidneys. Immediate surgery was suggested, followed by the usual protocol of radiation. At that time, our friend was in his mid-sixties, and happily married as well as deeply committed to the spiritual path. He was also physically very active, running every morning in the summer months and in the winter going to the Alps or Scandinavia for cross-country skiing. He asked the doctors what would happen to his manhood, and how long it would take him to be able to ski again (he had just booked a 3-week trip to Norway with that idea in mind).

The doctor's face turned as grim as the prognosis that he was going to give, regarding the likelihood of such recreational activities in the future. After the doctor had given his opinion, our friend thanked him and left, stating that he needed a second or even a third opinion. "But there is no time", the doctor warned, "we have to operate immediately." "No, we don't", our friend replied. "It is my body and my life, and I am going to find an alternative solution that satisfies me, because with what you are suggesting I should put myself through, I might as well be dead. What's the point of living, if you can't enjoy life?" He went to two more doctors who gave concurrent opinions. All the doctors became almost hopping mad trying to pressure and convince him by gravely pointing to his test results.

When our friend finally opted for a treatment, combining fasting, nutritional therapy and ozone therapy in a clinic in Germany, they declared him insane. And yet he lived for ten more years, quite content with his fate and taking several extended cross-country ski trips to Norway and other places. The therapy that he opted for required a lot of discipline. He had to completely change his diet (he had to drop his meat and potatoes), do regular fasts and visit the hospital for ozone treatments twice a year. Yet the disciplined regimen enabled him to get on with his life in the way he had wished for. He was not disabled or incapacitated, and when his time was up, he died a happy man. And why? Because he withstood tremendous outside pressure and trusted his own intelligence regarding the treatment that he finally chose. He mastered a challenging situation with a calm mind and an open and receptive heart.

The importance of following your own inclination at such a time cannot be overemphasized. So many times, we have seen close friends in similar situations that also chose intelligent therapies, which support the body and rebuild the immune system. However, after hardly the first timid attempts with these therapies, they get overwhelmed by hysterical relatives and workers in the health care industry who dissuade them from the person's own choice to instead engage in what they think best. Too often with extremely deleterious effects. We have seen too many body parts burned or chopped off of relatives, friends and acquaintances that could have easily been saved with an alternative more life enhancing therapy. Sometimes, knowing the general trend in the procedures of the health care industry makes people clam up and take no action. Hiding in a shell, however, will not make dis-ease disappear. Ultimately, it has to be faced. The question is, how.

Therefore, if you are seriously ill or have been suffering from severe mental and emotional pain, it is important to take proper action to support the body in what it can do best: heal itself. Even what appear to be solely emotional problems are sometimes connected to chemical imbalances in the body due to improper diet or stress, and are thus rooted in the physical. After addressing the cause of your affliction on an emotional and spiritual level, now with a calm mind and countenance, it is essential to take stock of your physical condition.

To understand what action you need to take, it helps to first understand how illness gets stuck and manifests in the body. Later we will go over the five key elements, necessary to recreate and then maintain excellent health. In the discussions in some of the previous principles, it has been emphasized how important it is to maintain an open attitude regarding the circumstances that arise in your life, no matter how challenging they are. Through the ability to maintain an open attitude, we then tend not to resist the uncomfortable feelings, which arise as a result of pain and suffering. By acknowledging them instead of resisting them, our feelings can then flow through the body/mind.

In other words, the energy of our emotional reactions does not get interrupted by resistance and end-up literally congesting or crystallizing in the body. The energy of the emotional reaction can simply flow through, leaving the cells of the body open and free. An example Paula often shares with her Reiki students, is the fact that strong emotions never cause a heart attack, it is our *resistance* to the strong emotions. which creates the real stress.

Emotions, are triggered by the mind in accordance to how we interpret each experience. If we label something mentally, "wonderful" or "terrible", we will have a "wonderful" or "terrible" emotional reaction to the situation. We slowly cease to be so troubled by the mind, if, on the other hand, we can see that there actually is no "good" or "bad", "fantastic" or "miserable", "exciting" or "boring". The mind loses the tight grip it has on us the moment we come to understand that life is just happening, and that it is the mind that interprets and labels events this or that way, according to its particular conditioning. When we understand this principle, even if the mind still reacts (which it inevitably will), we'll find ourselves less and less identified with the accompanying emotion that arises. Because we can perceive clearly how these reactions are all automatically activated, we cease to take ourselves (and others) so seriously.

The Buddha called this phenomena interdependent arising. Just try to imagine every person's body/mind's karma bumping up against everyone else's karma all at the same time. Some of the actions that result seem "terrible", some "wonderful", but as a matter of fact, it's only phenomena happening, with no real root cause. It is when we begin to label all these phenomena "good" or "bad" and assign causes to different events that the suffering begins. When we label or judge something, we immediately separate ourselves from it. We become the subject, the other person or circumstance, the object. In truth, there is nothing to judge, only to experience and feel.

From a higher order of understanding, we can begin to see how, in truth, "karma" does not actually exist – that it exists only on a relative level, in regard to the body/mind. We, as the vastness of consciousness or Buddha mind that has created the entire play, have no karma. However, karma is what we have to deal with on a day to day basis while we play unconsciously, identified with body/mind. Therefore, it pays to examine how this works for the individual on a physical level.

We have seen how, when we resist certain experiences or thoughts on a mental level, we then experience a corresponding reaction in the emotional body. When the reaction is intense, and especially if it is played out over and over again, it will crystallize in the physical body, creating a blockage in the area, which corresponds to the specific type of thought and its resulting emotion. For example jealousy, sadness and grief that are typically heartfelt emotions, usually get stuck in the heart area or upper chest. Breast tumors are often a result of these particular emotions. If a person has suffered sexual abuse, tumors or illness often manifest in the sexual organs or in the same general area. Another example is how unexpressed thoughts (all the things you wanted to say to your own personal petty tyrant but didn't) can literally get stuck in the throat and cause blockage and so on.

The various types of emotional release that are available through bodywork, have proven time and again, that thought forms do get stuck in the body. On the physical level we can see that the natural flow of cerebral spinal fluid is arrested wherever there is a blockage in the corresponding portion of the electronic or subtle body, which occurs whenever a natural law of the human mind is violated. What this means, is that when the ego (which is not the natural mind) identifies with something and resists it, a blockage occurs. Any thought pattern, word pattern or emotional pattern, tempered by resistance of any sort, will obstruct or warp the electronic structure of the body. Ego identification, whether "positive" or "negative", creates a certain resistance that lodges in the system and causes it to break down.

Saints and sages usually have a young and child-like face because they don't identify to the same degree the average person does. They often have a youthful aura about them as a result. Usually when they fall ill, it is because they are taking on the heavy energies of those around them to help relieve the suffering of humanity. When the previous Karmapa lay dying in a Chicago hospital, his doctors could not fathom how he remained alive. The body had disintegrated to such a degree (from taking so much on), yet still stayed alive, it was indeed amazing. The Karmapa's decision was a conscious one.

In most people however, the crystallization and resulting disintegration of the body happens unconsciously. Each organ of the body responds uniquely by a gradual reduction of life energy through the following process:

1. Mental resistance to any life experience results in energy blockage to the electronic body.

2. Blockage or warping in the electronic structure reduces the life force or electrical potential in corresponding areas; we then experience a one-to-one mapping with the other bodies (etheric, physical, etc.).

3. Crystallizations are the end result of suppressed thoughts, words or emotions – and will appear

in the body part, which does the suppressing. Each cell has its own resonant frequency that is affected by our resistance.

4. Crystals are composed of melanin protein complex, which exist inside the mytochondria of the cells of the body. Melanin reacts strongly to the energy of mental resistance or grasping (ego). It also acts like an organic computer chip full of stored memories that contain thought, word, and emotional patterns. Melanin complex thus acts as a self-perpetuating stimulus/response mechanism.

5. Crystallizations block the cerebral spinal fluid to the body part.

6. Consequently, nerve supply is diminished. Any blockage in cerebral spinal fluid will result in poor electrolyte circulation, and consequent inadequacies in regeneration.

7. Once nerve supply is diminished, circulation is diminished in that body part as well.

8. Lymphatic congestion is then registered in that body part. The spiral downward proceeds: Poor nutrient supply results, poor elimination of waste, undernourished cells dying in their own waste products, accumulation of waste products, tumor growth, etc...

9. The physical body thus becomes the outer manifestation of the inner patterns of thought, word, and emotion. ("As a man thinketh in his heart, so is he.")

Paula gleaned the above information from studying John Ray's groundbreaking work Body electronics years ago with Doug Morrison, Ray's primary student.

It is interesting to note that if you look at point 8 where the spiral downward into poor or ill health is described, you see most of the chronic conditions listed that afflict humanity. These are the root physical causes of disease. They are the exact opposite to the 5 key elements we need for psychological balance and good physical health. Below are listed the 5 chronic health problems and the 5 key elements to counter them:

1. Chronic Malnutrition	Eat healthy (minimally 50% raw foods)
2. Chronic Dehydration	Drink plenty of liquid (pure water, juices, herbal teas, etc.)
3. Chronic Elimination Problems	Fast, and do colonics periodically to thoroughly clean out the digestive/ eliminative tract and putrefaction of the colon.
4. Chronic Hypoxia (lack of oxygen)	Exercise in the fresh air and take periodic ozone treatments to detoxify
5. Chronic Resistance (to feeling & honestly perceiving what is really happening)	Cultivate wonderment as you allow yourself to feel from your heart.

Taking the 5 keys one by one, the first addresses the need to eat healthy foods that are rich in nutritional value. Paula has cured herself of three tumors with Gerson therapy or raw food diet. The raw live enzymes in uncooked food provide the basis for a healthy immune system. Before his death in 1959 at the age of 78, Dr. Max Gerson helped hundreds of patients cure themselves of advanced tuberculosis, heart disease, and cancer with his special raw food diet. His most famous patient was Dr. Albert Schweitzer, whom he cured of advanced diabetes when Schweitzer was 75.

Schweitzer then lived past 90. Both chronic and infectious diseases have been easily cured with raw food diet. It is simply a matter of discipline.

Diet can also have a profound effect on depression. In his time, one of the worlds leading authorities on nutrition and biological medicine, Dr. Paavo Airola had great success in treating both simple and clinical depression with nutritional therapy. He recommended a thorough examination by a competent doctor who would give tests for endocrine gland function, glucose tolerance, and mineral levels taken from the hair. Airola would then recommend certain nutritional supplements such as vitamins or minerals to compensate for the given deficiencies in the patient. Paavo Airola was also a great admirer of Dr. Benjamin Feingold's work with hyperactive children. Feingold found that the "trigger factors" of many behavior problems are directly related to poor nutrition. He found that highly processed, man-made foods with artificial colors and flavors, and other additives and preservatives are the culprit of hyperkinesis (hyperactivity). White flour and sugar also contribute to the condition, along with bad drugs, allergies, caffeine containing beverages such as soft drinks, chocolate, tea, and coffee.

Cola is one of the most deleterious beverages for human consumption, which taxes the naturally alkaline human body with high acidity. The high acidity in colas damages the stomach, pancreas, and liver, which then leads to peptic ulcers, diabetes, and severe lack of energy. To neutralize the high acidity the body summons a strong alkali-calcium hydroxide, which is present in bones. This rapidly neutralizes the invasive acid, preventing damage in other organs. However, repeated assaults lead to osteoporosis and osteomalcia, which have reached epidemic proportions in the developed world. All of the flavoring, coloring and preservative agents that cannot be thrown out by the human body, accumulate and often cause cancer. The high sugar content in cola and other soft drinks cause major over-stimulation of the glands in carbohydrate metabolism. This causes first a surge of energy as the carbohydrate rapidly gets metabolized, and then severe depression/exhaustion as important body chemicals are depleted. This constant cycle of repeated excitation and depression by heavy cola drinkers leads to mood swings, schizophrenia, lack of concentration and initiative, and in children often to hyperactivity.

The parents of 7% of America's school children are now being encouraged by the schools to counteract this hyperactivity by putting their children on Ritalin, a very serious and dangerous drug. But does it not make more sense to simply change their diet and give them the love they need? In some cases, the hyperactivity could also be alleviated, if teachers were allowed to work with a more interesting and challenging curriculum. A report by Jon Rappaport states: "800,000 American children are prescribed a cheap form of speed, called Ritalin. This drug is given for a bogus condition called ADD (attention deficit disorder). Ritalin eventually causes hyperactivity and depression, can cause acute withdrawal symptoms, and also an amphetamine-like psychosis. Ritalin makes drug addicts." It is sad when you realize all of this could be avoided by a simple, nutritional diet, free of chemicals and sugar.

Bad diet is a major contributing factor to degenerative disease. As far back as 1945, a publication of the U.S. Soil Conservation Service stated, " The United

States produce more food than any other nation in the world, yet according to Dr. Thomas Parran Jr., 40 % of the population suffer from malnutrition." The problem as he described it was due to the extensive depletion of minerals in the country's soil. One can only imagine how the soil is now, over fifty years later.

The bottom line from all the evidence, including the intriguing studies of the Hunza's who live high up in the mountains in Northern Pakistan, to well into their 100's, is that a moderate amount of raw food in the diet is essential. Some researchers have found that the ideal human diet should contain at least 75% raw food, and only 25% cooked. The average diet of almost everyone today is even worse than the simple opposite: 95% cooked and processed foods and only 5% raw. It is no wonder that degenerative diseases are rampant. The bottom line is, cooked food is dead food, even if it is vegetarian and has been prepared from organic ingredients that are free of chemical fertilizers and pesticides. Cooked food still lacks all the raw live enzymes the body really needs to sustain itself in good health. Ideally to maintain good health, you can grow your own garden and by giving it plenty of mineral rock dust, which can be obtained from certain rock quarries, you can also maintain a proper mineral balance. The results can be quite amazing.

After malnutrition, dehydration is the next issue to be dealt with. Most people in this busy world forget to drink enough, and what they do drink is often taxing to the kidneys. Caffeine, found in so many drinks such as colas, coffee, tea, and chocolate is highly toxic; especially when combined with all the other deleterious chemicals and white sugar as in soft drinks.

The purpose of proper amounts of liquid in the ⊔iet is to help the cells release the toxins stored in them, to flush the kidneys, and in general to keep a proper balance of water in the system. In the tropics where we live, it is especially important to drink constantly, as you tend to sweat just sitting in the heat of mid-day. Along the South Indian coastline, nature provides an excellent and nutritious drink in tender coconuts, which also gives back a lot of electrolytes. Unfortunately, today too many people fall prey to the misleading ad campaigns of soft drink companies and prefer drinks that do not flush their bodies of toxins, but instead fill them with more.

As an aside, our chronic dehydration can also be understood as a reflection of what is happening on a planetary scale. Deserts are expanding. Huge land-masses such as the Amazon basin are being deforest-ed. There is less and less good quality drinking water. The remaining water resources are compromised by pollution. All of these are large-scale signs of what we are doing to our own body. By not drinking enough as well as by drinking large amounts of toxic beverages, we are literally plugging up our own systems in the same way we are plugging up the earth with our own waste products and pollutants. Such an approach cannot but lead to an eventual system collapse.

The third key to good health is to maintain a clean eliminative tract. Although you may have regular bowel movements, if you eat a poor diet with a lot of fried or oily foods, white flour, sugar etc, your colon will tend to get clogged and sometimes bulge in places creating pockets, which store decayed food. This problem occurs to some extent to virtually every-one today, due to our highly refined and cooked diet.

The key to overcome this problem is to fast periodically, which Narayan and I do twice a year for 10 to 12 days. This eliminates build-up in the colon and helps to heal lesions. There are many good guides for fasting. Our favorite is Stanley Burrough's *'Healing for the Age of Enlightenment'*, where he gives excellent information on master cleanser, the lemon juice fast, which can be combined with either maple syrup or freshly pressed sugar cane syrup (absolutely no white sugar, or honey!). Paavo Airola is another favorite of ours. Three of his books give extensive and excellent information on fasting. They are, *How to Keep Slim, Healthy and Young with Juice Fasting, Are You Confused?*, and *There Is a Cure for Arthritis*, his fasting guide to cure rheumatoid arthritis.

Fasting is a practice that has been followed in many cultures for thousands of years as a way to detoxify the body/mind and also regenerate health - spiritually, psychologically and physically. Fasting was practiced in ancient Greece and Rome, and also by the Druids in Northern Europe. Native Americans fast during certain ceremonies, and records of fasting for spiritual and physical benefits have been found in Palestine, Egypt, Babylon, India, China and many other cultures. Hippocrates also was a great fan of fasting and recommended fasts up to seven days.

Dr. Otto Buchinger who directed two famous health spas in Germany, was cured of severe arthritis in both knees, which had crippled him as a young man, by a 28-day water fast. Basically, the way a fast works is that, deprived of food, the body begins to live off its own reserves. First it draws upon its stored glycogen (muscle sugar). After these are used up, certain enzymes in the bloodstream receive special attention and gain an intensified ability to dissolve hardened infusions. Because the increased fluids reach each and every cell, they soon create a liquefying action. Cholesterol and other deposits such as chlorine, calcium carbonate and uric acid simply melt away and are eaten by the body as a food. Usually, it takes three days for the faeces to stop eliminating, which is the time when the fast really begins to kick in and have a profound effect.

Fasting is not starving. The body always carries reserve stores of food that will last for quite some time, and in cases of obesity it lasts even longer. We have had several friends who have fasted for as long as forty (40!) days, with good results. Our experience is that a seven to ten day fast, at least once a year or preferably every spring and fall, helps to maintain excellent health. When the peristaltic action stops on the third day, it is a good idea to receive colonic treatments (a sophisticated enema) to help clean out the bowels. Also giving yourself an enema every other day during a fast can help as well.

The fourth key to good health is to keep the body oxygenated. In 1931, Dr. Otto Warburg won the Nobel Prize for medicine for discovering that the major cause of cancer is lack of oxygen in the cells. In 1944, he received another Nobel Prize for further research on the same subject. With such old, yet obviously esteemed research, is it not a bit strange that ozone therapy (which oxygenates the body) is not highly touted in the media? After all, it has a long proven track record as a cure for cancer and has been successfully used for over seventy years.

Perhaps the conclusion reached by German biostatistician Ulrich Abel in 1990 lends a clue. Abel published a book, *The Chemotherapy of Advanced Epi-*

thelial Cancer. Able had crunched numbers for many of the most important orthodox cancer studies in Germany but now he realized, after reviewing the literature on the subjects: "There is no evidence for the vast majority of cancers, that treatment with these (chemotherapy) drugs exerts any positive influence on survival or quality of life in patients with advanced disease." Abel was speaking of 70% - 80% of the cancers that kill people. At the time the book was published, the German news magazine *Der Spiegel* ran a major story on this issue. The American press blocked out Abel's evidence. No mention was made in the U.S. of his book. Follow the money trail, and you will understand, why.

It is also similar to why you never hear about ozone therapy. It is simply that ozone cannot be patented, and you cannot make the same unimaginable amounts of cash as can be made with the sacrosanct approaches of the medical establishment, whose research is mostly funded by the big drug cartels.

Ozone is O_3, a combination of O_2 and O_1. When used therapeutically, the O_2 gives support to the healthy blood cells, whereas the O_1 acts as a renegade that "eats up" toxic cells such as cancer, unhealthy bacteria, fungus, and yes, *all* viruses, including H.I.V.

In Cuba, which has been under an embargo for thirty years (including pharmaceutical drugs), simple and cheap ozone therapy has become the cure-all for a myriad of diseases. Many Americans and Canadians who suffer from cancer or H.I.V. now head for Cuba to be treated by this life-enhancing as well as life-saving cure. In fact, Cubans are on an average a lot healthier than the average Americans who are, and this is statistically proven, less healthy than Americans were sixty years ago. For example, according to government statistics, the U.S. spent over 3 trillion dollars on health-care in 1994, although people are overall, less healthy than they were in the 1930s!

Unfortunately these days, the health care industry doesn't seem to be doing much for maintaining good health. But there is a brighter side to this. The word about ozone in Cuba is spreading so fast that six more states now adopted ozone as a treatment for cancer and AIDS, making it a total of eleven states now supporting a therapy that is still very much suppressed in the media. But, we do know who owns the media. Just follow the money trail in the media and you will know why you don't hear about it in talk shows and documentaries.

Ozone is a natural phenomenon. It occurs, for example, after a thunderstorm. The fresh smell after lightening strikes, or of clothes dried on a line outside, is ozone. The way it is used therapeutically is quite simple. A tank of pure medical grade oxygen is hooked up to an ozone machine, consisting of basically two metal plates, one containing a negative charge and one containing a positive charge, through which the oxygen is directed. The charge acts to produce an extra molecule of oxygen, thus O_2 now becomes O_3.

There is a fine art to its application, as different doses are applicable to different conditions. An average treatment takes 3 to 20 minutes, with concentrations varying from 10 to 80 ug per milliliter. According to Ed McCabe, author of *Oxygen Therapies*, the maximum dosage is 5 parts ozone to 95 parts oxygen, with high concentrations used for disinfecting and cleansing, and low concentrations applied to promote skin growth and healing.

Ozone is used on staph infections, burns, fungal infections, radiation burns, herpes, gangrene, and a host of other ailments. It is administered in a variety of ways, through minor blood treatments; autohemo treatment (AHT); direct muscular injection; ozonated water; rectal insuflation; ozone baths; and ozone ointments. In Germany, where this therapy first appeared, currently 7,000 doctors use ozone, along with another 15,000 health care practitioners. Much of the research on ozone therapy over the past seventy years has been done in Germany, where millions of people have been treated with very positive results. Interestingly, even in Germany you don't hear about ozone in the media. Extensive information is however available on the Internet.

One of the easiest ways to promote the curative properties of oxygen in the blood, is through exercise. In a healthy body, exercise oxygenates the cells, and if you work up a good sweat, many toxins will also be discharged. Plenty of fresh air is a basic need and therefore essential. During the largest part of the evolution of the human body on this planet, there was approximately 38% oxygen available in the atmosphere. Now, in forests there is about 13-14%, and in large cities only 11%. Basically, we all suffer from hypoxia, or lack of sufficient oxygen, which is so necessary to nourish the cells properly and to throw off toxins. A series of three to five ozone treatments twice a year to maintain good health, is highly recommendable.

The fifth key to good health is to cultivate wonderment. A deep sense of awe straight from the heart sends out an impulse, which will loosen any withheld feelings. With wonderment, we develop a childlike openness to the real joy inherent in life. Instead of looking for a myriad of things to preoccupy and distract you from another empty day, you can take that sense of shallowness and confusion put forth by much of today's society, ...and can feel even this very confusion with wonderment.

One of the things that continues to create such underlying despair in today's world is the attitude of "been there, seen that, done that". This jaded information age that we live in has falsely lead us to believe that we know and have experienced everything, whereas in truth our knowledge is very limited, as is our range of experiences.

For example, there is a double-edged sword to the many very profound spiritual texts obtainable today. On the one hand, a lot of information that previously was only accessible to a student directly training with a master, is now available to the public. This allows many true seekers access to what was previously rare to discover in any given lifetime. These texts can thus act as pointers to where one needs to go to gain further depth. On the other hand, sacred texts that are now read out of simple curiosity, lead the reader to erroneously believe he or she "knows" everything about the subject. However, this is not so, as it really takes direct work with certain practices and the guidance of an experienced and selfless teacher to even begin to grasp certain teachings. Also, a lot of what is written on certain subjects is pure ego fluff and consequently, can only confuse the reader. Anything coming purely out of ego is always confusing, as it can only speak to and feed the ego, and the ego, by definition, is confusion.

For any spiritual practice to bear results, devotion is essential. To experience real joy in life also requires devotion, with a childlike sense of wonderment. This may seem very difficult to grasp for a western-trained mind (which today includes many Asians), but it is not impossible. It takes a shift in attitude. Purely and simply, a refusal to settle for less than the best life you can possibly have.

The next time you feel lost in confusion or in a deep sense of dissatisfaction, simply make the decision to stop looking outward for happiness, and instead resolve to explore the far reaches of inner space. Explore for yourself the happiness that is only waiting for you to notice. The process of rediscovery starts with simple wonderment. Instead of reacting with customary fear or resistance to your situation or state of mind (or both), begin to look at it with genuine awe, total wonderment. Put a smile on your face, even if it feels fake at first. Feel your smile *consciously*. Feel every part of your face and body smiling, as if each part had its own smiling mouth. Now open your mouth wide and say, "Ahhhh"!, as you stretch your arms wide.

With joyful curiosity, examine your situation as if you were reviewing a dream. "Wow, what an awesome scenario I have created", may be your response. Somehow you will be amazed at the intense shift in your perspective. It is difficult to describe in words exactly what you will experience. Suffice it to say, the overriding sense of dullness will be gone and something new will take its place.

At this point, it will be important to stay vigilant. Mind will want to interrupt with all your old patterns and take you back into "Dullsville". In case you notice this tendency, just bring your attention back to the superior intelligence of Heart, and from Heart once again, without judgment, be in total wonderment of the mind's manipulative games. Notice how a vigilant awareness can see right through the mind's games. This awareness is always with you. You only have to notice. You only have to feel. With vigileance, you can retrain yourself into a whole new way of being.

Regardless of circumstances, resolve to start each day in awe, and most of all, be in awe of your own joy, your own sadness, your own grief or anger, all of your mind's shenanigans. With delight, your compassion will grow, and healing and balance will surely be yours.

If you follow the principle of responsibility, take action, and choose therapies that support the 5 keys to good health, your well-being will increase exponentially. Here, we have dealt with only a few of our favorite healing modalities. Many more are easily available, such as: Allopathic; Ayurveda; Traditional Chinese Medicine; Bodywork; Chiropractic; Chelation Therapy (good for diabetes and heart problems); Homeopathy; Hydrotherapy; Nutritional Supplementation; Naturopathy; Western Herbal Medicine; and, believe it or not, Urine Therapy, which also gives remarkable results (it is like supplementing your body with your own internal antibiotic).

Our suggestions are in no way intended to limit your choices, but rather to inspire you to begin your own thorough research. If you are interested in more handy hints, look up the section on resources in the back of the book.

7

The Principle of Love

Love is caring. Love is tenderness. Love is also
passionate. When we embrace our troubles
tenderly like a mother caring for her child, our
troubles cease to be our enemies. They become
like our children whose misbehavior we accept
without judgment, whom we give space to expand
and grow until their resistance simply dissipates.
With enough practice and awareness, we can
learn how to dance the dance of enlightenment
with passionate self-abandon, even in the greatest
adversity. Through the embrace of such
passionate Love, everything is released.

Chapter 7

Embrace What Troubles You

So let the phenomena play.
Let the phenomena make fools of themselves by themselves.
This is the approach.

- Chögyam Trungpa

In previous discussions it has been pointed out how illness or discomfort persist when we resist them. One of the best ways to complete this cycle of resistance is to simply embrace wholeheartedly whatever it is you have resisted.

It is like a mother embracing her newborn child who cries out in resistance to its new environment. In your case, it may be your illness, depression, or common frustration that needs to be attended to. It needs to be soothed and loved until it can simply dissipate. Everything is transitory in this world. Nothing lasts forever, including illness and negative mental states. By mothering ourselves, by energetically giving to ourselves the love we need, by allowing ourselves to cry, to take a day off work just for ourselves, we support the healing process. Time off to further shift our attitude once we have begun to take action, is also very helpful during challenging periods.

When you understand that all the circumstances you attract are somehow connected to your own actions, you can be grateful that the effect of a particular action is now complete. All actions invariably give rise to corresponding effects, and these can carry over for lifetimes like the previous example of the Buddha's headache. When we resist the effects that befall us, the effects of those same actions will only increase and multiply. We end up simply attracting the same result (effect of a previous action) with a new face or slightly different circumstance, all equally uncomfortable. To complete this potentially repetitious cycle, it behooves us to graciously accept the adverse circumstance, which has arisen in our life, as the wake up call that it is. A creative and liberating response to adversity is to say, "Thank you, universe, for bringing this challenge now, so that I may complete the lesson that I obviously need to learn."

It is important to remember that you never experience the effects of an action that you haven't committed. In other words, everything you experience is a direct reflection of all your previous actions. All of us have committed what we normally call "good" and "bad" actions, although there truly is no "good" or "bad". There are really only ignorant or conscious acts - actions committed while sleep-walking through existence and actions committed in the state of wakefulness. Because we have engaged in both positive and negative actions for many lifetimes we never really know when either cycle will appear.

We can prepare ourselves for cycles of adversity by openly welcoming them for the teaching they can bring, and the ultimate strengthening effect they can have on our psyche. Paula remembers how, years ago, while visiting her teacher, that an insight arose, which she then shared with him. "I feel very blessed by the tremendous adversity I have had to face in my life. It has helped me wake up enough to be able to find you." He sort of winked and smiled at her with his knowing grin.

Today looking back, it is clear that it was not so much the adversity, which helped her along the way. What really made a difference was the attitude she was able to foster while dealing with it. Somehow some fundamental faith that basically all is well with the world, has always been there, coupled with a tiger-like fierceness and determination that ultimately nothing is insurmountable.

On some deep level (although not always on the surface), there is an awareness that "I am ultimately responsible for all of the circumstances, and especially their effects, that I attract in my life." When we have this attitude of responsibility toward the experiences we attract in our lives, it becomes much easier to accept and thus embrace them. Adversity then can be used as a support for purifying unwholesome actions, in effect clearing up old karma in such a way that it does not then have to repeat itself. When we can remember that all the deeds we have ever committed never fail to produce results, we will tend to choose more carefully in the present, the actions we will engage in.

In regard to the previous theme of taking action, for example, have you so far allowed others to make decisions for you, or have you responsibly done your own research and made your own decisions? Do you unquestioningly "buy into" your doctor's story, or any other so-called "expert", or do you also listen to your own inner knowing? Are you a fighter? Do you want to live? Really? And what for? What do you want to accomplish? – The decisions you make now will determine your actions, and your actions will ultimately create more karma, "good" or "bad". Only you can decide what it will be.

In the last analysis, attitude will always be more important than the circumstance you find yourself in. For example, you can have two children who both grew up in the same unfortunate circumstances, yet one later in life becomes happy and successful, while the other turns out to be hateful and revengeful. What makes the real difference between the two, is the attitude.

A positive, responsible attitude wins every time, and it is tested and honed in the fire of adversity. One who makes it through perilous circumstances successfully, most likely has had enough practice in other lifetimes to realize that going for the negative is not an option. The only option is to accept the Grace, which is waiting to take you across the perilous ocean of Samsara (illusion).

The fact of the matter is that Grace is always within us, just waiting for us to notice. It is available to all equally, but not all choose to access it. Perhaps because you are reading this, it is your time to do so. If you somehow sense this, but are having a hard time reaching out to accept Grace, perhaps the following little anecdote from Paula's life in her own words will inspire you.

"When I was thirteen, like many children at that age, I became depressed and badly disgruntled with my life. I was unhappy at school. Except for a rare few, I felt most of my teachers were dull and insensitive, not to mention uninspiring. Most of my fellow students seemed to be in a stupor of inanity, effected by peer pressure to tow a certain fashion line or follow certain nonsensical behavior. I couldn't seem to find any friend that I could relate to on a deeper level, something I really craved. For months it went on like this until I became quite desperate. I became very depressed, and I wondered why I was alive. What was my purpose for living? I became so desperate, I finally approached my mother (who was busy with three younger children) and told her I needed some help, that I felt very suicidal. She immediately realized how serious my plight was. Perhaps, she was already suspicious. She inquired and found a psychologist whom some friends recommended.

As it turned out, the man I went to speak to was very helpful. I will never forget him, for he saved my life. His treatment was so simple, I only needed to see him once or twice. He basically told me that I was sane and that indeed what I experienced was true, most people are totally asleep and it is hard to make real contact. He told me not to worry, that in a few short years I'd be finished with school and out on my own, and could then make my own decisions. He assured me that there are a few sane people around and that I would find them, once I could determine my own direction in life. He suggested in the meantime that I just concentrate and focus on what really interested me, and not to waste a minute on the nonsense of others.

I took his advice to heart. This dear man I will never forget. I have followed his advice my entire life, and with excellent results. The sad part about it is, I shudder to think what would have happened to me today, if the same feelings were overwhelming me. With the prescription feel — good drugs now incredulously advertised on television, I might have been encouraged to join the growing army of the numbed out, but "happily coping" innocents (whose ranks according to government statistics are swelling at about 1/2 million per month). It is unlikely that I would have reached my full potential.

Does anyone ever consider that it is perhaps a very sane reaction to have such bad feelings, when you consider the things that are going on now? We happen to be entering one of the densest stages of kali yuga, the degenerate era according to Eastern cosmology – yet which can be an opportune time to wake up from Samsara, if you know how to use skillfully, the powerful energies frozen in the density. And to do so skillfully, involves trusting your feelings.

In other words, if you feel bad, there is *most likely a good reason*. And the only way through uncomfortable feelings is to go right through them to the other side. The technique is elementary: simply put ALL your attention, ALL your focus on your feelings, *without trying to make them go away*. Do this every time you notice uncomfortable feelings, and again check your motive. This cannot be overemphasized. If you try this technique out with even the slightest unconscious intention to make your uncomfortable feelings go away, you will never get through them. The motive to make something go away is *resistance*. So, the feelings will simply grow stronger. They will *persist*.

The secret is to develop a strong attitude of acceptance, to literally embrace your feelings, each time they arise, with a sense of wonderment. Dive right in with full determination, and put all of your attention on them, like a scientist exploring inner space, with total awe and wonderment. Then check out what happens. Feel what happens. You will be amazed.

The solution is so simple. It is a matter of doing what we do naturally feel. Yet it is the very thing we are taught by society to suppress. In the present era, this trend toward suppression of genuine feelings is growing stronger every day. Such repression is pure and simple resistance to waking up. I felt these things as a young teenager. Because of such a wise counselor, however, I received a major reality check. He simply told the truth, the hard truth. The gift he gave me was to help me face life as it is, with all its ups and downs, with all of its harshness. You embrace something by knowing it for what it is. It then no longer remains outside of you. It becomes a part of you that you understand.

Unfortunately, I don't remember my counselor's name. He was a tiny man who looked like Vincent van Gogh, with red hair and a beard. Wherever you are, my angel, I send you a thousand hugs for challenging me. For letting me know that my suicidal feelings were only my heart crying out for what is real, and that these feelings were there to show me that I had reached my bottom line. After such a reality check, I could never settle for second best. I realized then that it was clearly up to me and no one else to discover what was right for me. Fortunately, I had the Grace to be able to heed the counselor's challenge.

The fortitude I gained from this brief interaction helped me through my own brother's suicide two years later, partly due to the administration of steroid drugs by a doctor, which caused severe depression. He had also gone to a counselor, but was not so lucky to find someone as perceptive and empathetic as I had. His counselor had actually only further provoked his problems. My brother's violent death made me realize how short life really is, and that there truly is no time to waste on the advice of fools. Because of my brother's death who I felt closest to at the time, I then had to face the intensity of despair. I had no illusions about life by then, so I was able to finally come out on the other side.

From this experience, I learned that I could face anything, even death if I had to, for ultimately there is no running away. I realized then that my sadly misguided brother would just have to come back again and start over where he left off. In the end, I embraced it all. Death. Life. All the sorrow, and finally all the joy.

Ultimately, life exists so we can feel and experience it. Adversity is really just the opposite side of felicity. The two are only different sides of the same coin. When you expect that there will always be cycles of each, it becomes easier to embrace them. Adversity will always be uncomfortable, but the secret is, we don't necessarily have to suffer over our discomfort with it.

Instead of trying to wriggle free from a difficult situation, if we just slow down and actually sit still with all the feelings that arise and really focus on them, instead of resisting them, a solution will inevitably unfold. However, don't allow "looking for a solution" to distract you from the feelings until they are complete. Rather than complicating things with impatience and struggle, foster a positive attitude of "hum, what an interesting challenge" or "what can I learn from this?".

Ultimately, to embrace whatever life brings our way with openness and love takes the suffering out of any imbalance or disease. With such an attitude, all of life becomes self-liberating. Then, we can mentally step back, yet fully engage in and allow the phenomena to play. The moment we stop identifying with all phenomena, including most of our own and all other body/minds, the phenomena begins to make fools of themselves by themselves.

8

The Principle of Devotion

Our true needs are our calling in life. They have drawn us here into this existence. The way to fulfill them is to honor them. When we discover what we truly need and ask for it, our life's purpose can be fulfilled. Also, when we have the courage to ask, our heart opens and allows us to receive our good. The key element here, is devotion. Whims and fantasies never inspire devotion. Only our heartfelt need can. However, to uncover our genuine need, we also have to learn how to fulfill our little needs. If fulfilled wisely, they will lead us to the devotion inherent in our heartfelt need.

Chapter 8

Ask for What You Need

The Lover is the Beloved.
The subject of your search is the object,
And so you will never find it.
The only way to love Self
Is to BE IT.

— Papaji

Asking for what you need, although it may seem like a passive act, is actually a direct way to advance toward your life's true purpose. It is thus important to be very clear about what you ask for. Sometimes we chase after desires that are wholly irrelevant to this purpose. Life then takes us down a blind alley. We can tell we have taken such a diversion when we experience a growing sense of unhappiness. When we then ignore this unhappiness for too long, it can turn into despair. Despair is only the Heart calling us, guiding us out of the dark and into the light.

When a nagging sense of dissatisfaction becomes prolonged, it is high time to turn your attention inward and consult with the only one who knows your true course — the superior intelligence of Heart. It feels your need for it is not separate. It is aware of the veil of ignorance that shields your divine longing for your own Beloved with the false cover of illusory despair, a despair caused by all the actions you have taken, lead along by the desires of your mind.

Unlike the desires of the Heart, the desires of the mind are fantasy yearnings, programmed into you by the TV screen of Samsara, your illusory world. Such desires will keep you in physical and emotional suffering and on the constant rounds of life, death and rebirth.

When you chase after the myriad of desires, which arise in the mind, you remain in a continuous state of unconsciousness. Instead you can drop the suffering of karma, the consequences of your actions, when you rid your mind of all desire *for or against anything*.

From deep within you can allow life to take its natural course. You do not need to deny yourself the basics of life, by becoming a staunch "renunciate", who is *against* everything, or the equally unconscious opposite polarity of the hedonist. Instead you can unveil the true bodhisattva (enlightenment being) within, who is neither attached nor detached — who simply IS. In total wonderment, you observe the rise and fall of your own attachment and aversion, as you notice how everything is actually just happening. No real cause; no effect; no reason; just happening.

The body/mind automatically knows what to do in every situation anyway, even if that involves asking for directions. When you identify as Awareness, rather than an isolated body/mind, you can participate fully in life without suffering over it. No longer identified as a separate entity or ego-self, but as Awareness, you perceive that You are not in the body, but your "body" - and all other "bodies" - are inside of You.

When you have this direct experience of reality, you "don't sweat the small stuff". Your life becomes balanced between the major tasks at hand and also of giving yourself the small pleasures of life when the feeling arises.

Paula remembers one humorous incident a few years ago, which serves to illustrate this point. At the time she attended Satsang ("sitting in truth") five days a week with her master Poonjaji, or Papaji, as he was known to many. Satsang is usually a time of sitting in silence, and often followed by a question and answer session on spiritual topics, usually regarding self-inquiry. Satsangs with Papaji always were a very lively affair, and something to look forward to. As Paula states:

"One day as we came out of silence, Papaji motioned to one of his helpers and whispered in his ear. A couple of people then proceeded to bring out a TV set, and without a word, Papaji settled down to watch a cricket match. Weakened by old age, the effects of diabetes and barely able to walk, this had become his favorite pastime at home. Several of the male devotees would go over and sit with him during these matches. Never before, however, had he done so in the "sacred space" of Satsang Hall. I watched the faces of a group of Americans who had just arrived, obviously expecting this very "holy man" to conduct himself in a specific guru-like fashion. The look of dismay was so striking that some of us couldn't help ourselves and fell into hysterical laughter. Most of us knew that the "real teaching" he shared was beyond words. But on a purely physical level, on that particular day, he obviously needed a break."

All of us need the simple pleasures in life. To some it may be a walk in nature. To others it may be going to the ballpark for a game, or to a movie. It may be active sports or one of the many arts. The Dalai Lama, for example, is known to enjoy fixing mechanical things in his spare time. Whatever it is that gives a sense of joy or evokes peace is necessary to balance out job stress and even spiritual practice. Narayan and I enjoy body surfing several days a week when we are at home, and occasionally treat each other with various forms of bodywork.

One of the things which is happening in today's busy world, is that people are becoming even more overly obsessed with work and never find time for a break. The fear of not being able to pay off huge credit debts keep many from taking important time off to relax and regenerate. Others become workaholics to avoid facing themselves or hollow relationships at home.

At some point, we all have to take stock and assess what is really important in our lives. A good exercise is to imagine with full conviction that you only have one week left to live, and then decide what you want to do with that week. Then do the same exercise, imagining you have only 24 hours left to live. What would you do? Once you decide, then go out and do it! When time is of the essence (as they state in all the credit agreements that you sign in the course of your adult life!) we become suddenly very clear about what is really important. When you actually follow through and go out and do it, you begin to take your power back. It then becomes easier to ask for what you genuinely need.

The universe is abundantly rich in resources. Do not become discouraged, if one or two of these sources have not come through for you. If some idea or goal is really close to your heart, you will find a way. Chances are however, when you assessed the things you would want if you had only 24 hours to live, they were probably very simple. Yet, they are most likely the very things you don't give to yourself, because they always seem accessible. Such things as spending *quality* time with your spouse or children, are necessary every day, even if it has to be short. Finding time to meditate, sitting quietly by yourself. These are the things that keep us sane as human beings, in a world that these days, is often out of balance.

The path to sanity is also the path to enlightenment. Enlightenment basically means to be fully awake to who we truly are; to be able to see through all of our patterns and simply embrace them. To really wake up, take help from others who are also on the path.

Earlier we mentioned that bodhisattva means "Enlightenment Being". Bodhisattva also means a "being on the path to enlightenment". On some level all of us are bodhisattvas. So, it is important to be aware of the pitfalls that society places in your way. These are the very things that make us fall ill, or become depressed or frustrated. They are what make you afraid to ask for what you need. And all of these things come under one main category, and that is doubt.

When you doubt yourself, when you doubt the truth of who you really are; when underneath it all, your superficial success is due to the drive to prove, that you are really "good enough", the pure bliss of genuine happiness cannot be felt.

In all the various countries of the world where we have taught seminars and retreats, there seems to be one common theme, which underlies all the unconscious patterns and which can be summed up in one phrase: "I am not worthy". This one underlying belief is at the root of all the insanity we experience.

A person who feels unworthy can play out the extreme Napoleonic complex of a tyrant in order to compensate for feeling small, or its opposite polarity, the "poor little waif" or "doormat". Both of these and all of their variations in between are a lie. Each of us is neither grand nor unimportant. Together we make up the sum total of humanity, with each body/mind playing its purposeful role. All are worthy, and each has the right to life, liberty and the pursuit of happiness. Where we get lost, is when we become programmed to believe that it is our right to have these things handed to us on a platter from an outside source. This only creates unhealthy dependency on outside agencies and takes away our own intrinsic self-sufficiency.

The universe has provided everything we'll ever need. It is up to us to turn inside, and from our Heart, ask for it. Only we can feel what we need, not some outside source that tells us we should have a certain kind of house, car, and 2.2 children. If that is what we truly want, it is up to us to seek it out and take appropriate action to make it happen. When we follow our own Heart, and trust it with the Devotion it deserves, miracles can happen. If we ask for anything only with our mind, the universe will not respond in the same way. When we can let go of our head, however, the distractions of fantasy yearnings, manufactured in the mind (and in the mind of Madison

Avenue), will fade away. The mind then becomes the helpmate of the Heart.

When you can say to another from your Heart, "I need you", a joyful response ensues, unlike the clinging mental neediness, which only pushes others away. Your calling in life is your Heart's quest. Honor it with devotion, and it will set you free.

9

The Principle of Enlightenment

As much as enlightenment is not a goal, but one continuous reality, health and balance are our natural state, not something we need to strive for. Only when we appear to have strayed from our nature, do we appear to need to strive to regain our health and balance. Enlightenment permeates all of existence. It is ever present. We cannot find it outside of ourselves or in an imaginary future because it is already here. It is simply a matter of receiving It, through surrender to That, which we truly Are.

Contd.

Contd.

In the same way, on the deepest level, we cannot even seek and find health and balance, as they are already given. It is through openness and receptivity, that our natural state of balance is realized. This is basic sanity and the end of all strife.

Chapter 9

Be Open and Receive

Not knowing how near the Truth is
We seek it far away – what a pity!...
We are like him who,
In the midst of water,
Cries out in thirst so imploringly.
We are like the son of a rich man
Who wanders away among the poor...

— *Zen Master Hakuin*

To experience balance in mind and body it is necessary to understand the essential oneness in nature. There is a constant ebb and flow in the cycle of things: the tides; time; weather; and even the human body – all giving the appearance of two forces working against each other. In truth, the two are one complete whole, such as the governing and functioning vessels, the two main meridians or energy lines, which flow around the circumference of the human torso. One begins at the perineum, runs up the spine to the top of the head, and down to the roof of the mouth. The other starts at the tip of the tongue and runs down the center of the front part of the body, again to the perineum. A closed circuit is created when the tip of the tongue touches the roof of the mouth. One full circle of continuously flowing energy, with no real beginning and no end. The human Heart has a direct experience of this oneness.

It is only when we try to comprehend oneness with the mind that confusion arises. The mind can only comprehend things by comparison to something else. To understand cold, it calls on the experience of hot; to understand light, it calls on its seeming opposite, dark; and so on. The mind can only imagine two things coming together, calling this juxtaposition "unity". Real Oneness is beyond its ken.

Because of the human mind's belief in itself as a separate "self" or ego, it automatically sets itself up as a subject to which everything else then becomes an object. The separate self is a false premise on which all other false premises are based. In truth all these little egos that see themselves as separate are nothing but rollicking waves on the ocean of Consciousness. They seem separate because the five senses of the body/mind convince the ego that this is so. However, the waves are all very much the ocean – in a temporary state of flux.

Quantum physics tells us that this is so: that we are not separate and that there is no solid matter. According to its view, all of creation is a myriad of vacillating frequencies of energy, which take on the appearance of a variety of forms. It is just as if there is one resourceful playwright, simultaneously dividing herself up into a multitude of characters in one great cacophonous yet actually harmonious spectacle, called life.

Only the Heart can appreciate such a wondrous concoction of elements, all existing in full accord yet simultaneously appearing to diverge. When the human mind finally surrenders to its source; when we become still and experience the silence, which is our true nature – the silence, which is the mother of all sound – a new symphony is heard: Existence, Consciousness, Bliss. The source of all genuine surrender is the ego, bowing down to its Source.

For most of us, "Source" is just a concept and so many platitudes. Somehow, we sense it, we yearn for it, but it constantly eludes us. What is this great joy? What is this great bliss that all the sacred scriptures speak of? Why can't I have it? Why do I have to suffer? Source is so close. Yet, we are like fish in the sea crying out for water, or like an adolescent tiger brought up by donkeys, who when he first sees himself in all his majesty reflected in a pond, roars out in terror, bewildered by his own might.

There is a story told about a man who owned a gold mine in Africa. He dug for many years until he hit pay dirt. For a couple of years he prospered until the particular vein he had found ran out. He dug for a while in different directions and finally frustrated, decided to sell out. The first thing the new owner did was to hire an expert geologist who examined the site thoroughly. Using his knowledge, he predicted that if they dug in a particular direction for so many feet they would probably reach another vein. The new owner followed the geologist's advice, ...and hit the mother lode.

This story conveys the importance of patience and perseverance. So often for our ordinary everyday happiness, what we need or what we are looking for is right in front of us. Many times we fail to notice because we don't take that little extra time or effort, which could tilt the scales in our favor. This unwillingness to be vigilant and to exert ourselves, for many, creates a lot of unnecessary unhappiness and frustration. It prevents us from receiving what actually already has been given to us, and illustrates how skillfully we sabotage ourselves.

Another parallel we can draw, is how casually we treat our own resources, which are inherent in our own body/mind. Many people don't draw on them at all, and the few who do, most often don't know how to derive their full potential. Even though some may be a little more venturesome, they usually only scratch the surface and content themselves with their obvious blessings, whereas the deeper blessings remain untouched and go to waste.

It is the spiritual teacher or guide who can help us reveal our most precious treasure, which for all but a few is not even heard of, let alone experienced and integrated. Most humans have no idea of the possibility we have, to fully awaken while in this human body. We actually have direct access in every moment to the Truth of who we are and to the ultimate health and unimaginable well-being of lasting peace and liberation. The ones who do have a glimpse, if they are discerning, rely on a little help from an "outside expert". They seek a spiritual guide to help them proceed in the right direction, so that when they dig, they can finally hit the inner gold of true recognition – their own Buddha nature, or Self.

Giving up all of the ego's demands and commands, the reins are now given back to Source (which never really relinquished them in the first place). The realization dawns that the great mother Heart has been there all along, emanating Grace, humming her celestial song, just waiting to be received by her recalcitrant child. As we surrender to her loving embrace, inseparable from our own Heart, all of our doubt fades away.

When we let go of our misguided ideas of being unworthy, true healing occurs. Whether the body lives or dies is then of little consequence, as it has nothing to do with the true healing of our alienation from ourselves. When we surrender to our innermost power, we also surrender lifetimes of bondage, so that we can simply Be. Unfettered of the heavy shackles of ego-mind, the body very often heals more quickly. However, not knowing the body/mind's karma, on the physical level the end result can never be predicted.

What is known, is that when the ego surrenders to its own Heart energetically, a profound healing takes place. We begin to feel lighter. Unburdened of a heavy load, all of creation can then flow through us. We discover that what we were seeking all along was the very Source of the seeker, our own Heart. As the seeker dies, finally embraced by Itself, a new frequency is released – the frequency of Freedom, the frequency of Love. We can simply Be, open and in tune to the universe within our own Heart.

Chapter 10

Introduction
to the 40-Day Program

Because our powers of observation
are usually not well developed,
we are often blind to our suffering.

— *Tarthang Tulku*

The Perfect Motivation for Daily Practice

What better motivation for committing yourself to doing this program than to discover the perfect wellness, which already dwells in you, albeit unnoticed! What better motivation than to include all your loved ones and eventually all living beings in your desire for health, happiness and freedom from unnecessary restriction and suffering!

The 40-Day Program is designed to hone your power of self-observation to the point that you can deeply feel and understand yourself from the inside out. It is designed to help you rediscover and maintain a special kind of knowing, similar to what we usually call intuition. This form of knowing or intuiting is not a gift that only a few people have. It is something that in one form or another we all share. It can be cultivated and put to use. If you pursue this program, your powers of self-observation will increase and you will cease to be blind to your suffering. Rather you will have the chance to learn from it and even transform it into the underlying bliss that is concealed within the core of all pain.

The starting point and main focus throughout the program is your own experience. However, once you become sensitized to feeling yourself and the unconscious driving forces that are constantly shaping and molding your life, you will automatically start to notice what is happening in your loved ones and in the people all around you in a very new light. In other words, through focusing on your own feelings you will also become more open to the feelings of others. Through becoming more self-observant, your perception will expand in regard to both yourself and others. You will discover the natural wisdom and compassion residing in your heart.

As you continue with the program, all of this will unfold quite naturally and spontaneously, like a flower opening to the morning sun. So you don't really have to concern yourself with how to achieve a particular end. You can trust that as long as you stay committed to exploring your own truth, all will be unveiled naturally.

It is essential to remind yourself daily of the interconnectedness, in fact inseparability of self and others on a deeper level. This is why in the texts that you recite daily, references to this truth are included. They serve as an ongoing intimation to the web of life that we share with all beings and to counteract the inveterate tendencies of the ego.

The 40-Day Program

The best way for you to experientially explore the nine themes of the program to Absolute Wellness is by repeating each of them four times for a total of thirty-six days, and then by adding four days of silent meditation. A 40-day setting affords you the rare privilege of becoming more fully acquainted with yourself.

Four repetitions of each step, in four consecutive 9-day rounds are suggested for a reason. Usually the first 9-day round will serve to familiarize you with the structure and content of the program. It will get you started and inspire a first inner response, which in many cases will remain unnoticed because your main focus is on getting your bearings in a completely new and unfamiliar environment. The second 9-day round, very often will both deepen your self-understanding as well as bring up your inevitable resistance to new insights and feelings, which begin to bubble up. Round three is crucial, as it affords you the opportunity to let go of your resistance. In round four you have finally dug deep enough to trust the flow of the process and reap its first substantial benefits. Finally, the four days of silent contemplation at the end are fundamental to anchoring and distributing the benefits throughout your body/mind.

It is suggested that you follow this 40-day format when you first start working with the material presented in the book. However, if you want to take up your exploration again at a later time, you may do so in a different format of your choice. You may choose any multiple of nine, like 18, 27 or even 108 – or just nine days as a refresher course. However, even if you choose a format other than the 40-day structure, al-

ways conclude with several days of silent contemplation as outlined for days 37-40. The longer your
exploration lasts, the longer should also be the period
of quiet meditation at the end.

There is great wisdom in repeating a practice, as
each repetition will automatically reveal new facets of
yourself. At the same time, the cleansing effect of this
self-exploration gets intensified. Just recall, how many
years you have sleepwalked through your life already. To counteract this tendency, a disciplined effort for a number of days without interruption is
necessary. The choice is yours. But chances are, that
you will need to get to know yourself and to learn to
feel yourself a whole lot more, before you can fully
embrace life with the Love that you essentially are.

It is not wise to turn this program into an obligation. It is not helpful to venture into this type of self-
exploration out of guilt or because you believe you
have to. Self-exploration is not a religion of "dos" and
"donts". It happens because you feel inspired, because you feel the pull to greater awareness, health
and happiness. Only commit to it because you feel
that it will bring you joy.

The Basic Structure of the Daily Practice

Every session on each of the 9 Principles of Self-
Healing has five distinct steps which have to be
followed diligently to bring about the intended effect.
The subsequent explanations describe the function of
each step and why its implementation is important for
the success of the entire program. As a concerted
whole over time, they serve to develop and strength-
en considerably your powers of self-observation as

well as your intuition about what is appropriate for you in the present moment.

Step 1

The first step is to be quiet for a few moments. To be able to focus on the issue you wish to explore and contemplate, it is advisable that you first soften the impact of your normally busy mind and relax. It is essential to really be with yourself and feel yourself, to step out of your mind and into your heart.

The approach you follow to tune in with this detached mode of focusing is totally up to you. You may want to assume a specific posture as if to formally meditate. Some may want to sit comfortably on their favorite spot in the apartment or house, or out on the porch, in a rocking chair or on that recliner, wherever you feel most protected. You may even want to turn on some soft, meditative background music for five minutes to help you focus and let go of any excess mental agitation. If you don't opt for music, it will help to open your senses to whatever outside sounds are there: the far away traffic noise, the birds in the front yard, the rain on the roof, the wind in the trees. You don't need to concentrate on them, just notice them.

The only thing you absolutely don't want to do, is turn on the boob tube, or some early morning radio talk show. This would inevitably draw your attention away from yourself and defeat your purpose, as you would become distracted.

Again: the purpose for starting out with a few moments of silence is to help you focus on yourself: your own sensations, feelings and concerns. When we sit in silence, the thoughts and feelings we have been ignoring come up. Sometimes initially, the mind begins to chatter more forcefully in order to cover these feelings. If your mind goes into chatter mode, simply allow it. Observe its shenanigans peacefully in total equanimity. The more you focus on your thoughts, *allowing* them to be there, the quieter your mind will become. If you resist them, they will persist.

It's only practical, if you really want to listen into yourself, to explore what might be wrong, to be silent and allow whatever is there to be revealed. Therefore the first step is to become silent and to keep quiet.

Step 2

This is the actual session of self-inquiry. At this point, suggestions are made and commands are given to help invoke unconscious memories, which need to be brought into conscious awareness so that they cease to control you. Working with commands helps you to access unconscious mind directly. Whereas a question format would only encourage the mind to ruminate and analyze. This would not help you to become more aware of things as they really are. At this time, you also need to turn off any background music so that you can focus without distraction on the feelings that arise.

In order for things to shift, you first need to become aware of the underlying causes that have created what you are currently experiencing. With this awareness, you will begin to intuit the steps you will need to take, to turn your situation around. To achieve this aim, is the purpose of your self-inquiry. It can best be accomplished in a state of relaxed receptiveness, which ensures that your heart is open. An open heart will facilitate your ability to feel.

Step 3

Here, you will anchor the insights gained in step 2. You are asked to read three times out loud to yourself the short statement given as a summary for your self-exploration and inquiry. This will help you to anchor your own insights. It will also help you to recondition your mind and attune it to a more wholesome and less self-destructive pattern. It is very important that you read your statement three consecutive times. If you do this, you will avail yourself of the power of an ancient esoteric law that states that whatever you say or enact three times, will actually become true. Repeating the statement three times will leave no room for doubt in your mind as to what your intentions are. For that particular instant, you will be free of doubt and worries. Later you will be able to expand this awareness and stay free of doubt and worry for longer than just a fleeting moment.

Step 4

It is very important that you also end your session in silence. This will help you integrate your new insight and awareness. Just sit for a few short moments very quietly and integrate the gift that you have just given to yourself. You don't need to unnecessarily drag out step 4, until the silence becomes oppressive. Simply stop and go about your business the instant you feel a sense of completion.

Step 5

Write down the insights from the day's exploration in a separate notebook, which you will keep solely for the purpose of the 40-Day Program. This way, you will have continued access to your insights and realizations, which you might otherwise quickly forget.

The Progression through the Nine Themes

There is a logical order to the nine themes, and it behooves us to understand their sequence so that we will know exactly where we are going. To have an initial grasp of the inherent logic of the program will support you in its day-to-day application.

The first four themes are designed to hone our powers of self-observation. Focusing our awareness on them, will make us more receptive and also more perceptive. This is essential. If we intend to heal ourselves, we have to first be in a position to notice what is going on within our own body/mind. We also need to get a sense of the underlying challenges and trends in our lives that we normally prefer not to address, but instead keep sweeping under the carpet. Exploring these themes will reveal to us our unconscious suffering, and its root cause.

This serves as the basis for themes 5 through 8 through which we train ourselves to act in new and different ways. As they are designed to allow for the creation of more wholesome habits and attitudes, these themes gently guide the body/mind toward a more healthy and realistic way of being in the world.

Finally comes the ultimate challenge, theme 9. Here, the receptivity, gained in steps 1 through 4, are combined and integrated with a new way of being in the world, gained in steps 5 through 8. This integration allows for an all-encompassing receptivity, the ability to participate fully in life, which enables us to receive whole-heartedly what we truly need at any given moment.

The Commentaries

When you begin to "de-condition" your mind and introduce new and healthy ideas to replace old engrained patterns, the new ideas need to be reiterated constantly. Most of the time your consciousness is not in focus. Normally thousands of thoughts are passing through your mind at random. These are not original thoughts, but derive from past memories and future plans. As long as you remain attached or identified with these thoughts out of habit, they will constantly grab your attention and drain your energy, always reinforcing the past conditioning even further. Initially, you need to make a concerted effort to focus on new thoughts, when you intend to change them.

As you begin each theme every day, and before you begin Step One, sitting in silence, it is helpful to read the accompanying commentary. The themes, which were discussed at length in each of the nine chapters, and which are brought up in Step Two of the program each day, are again expanded on in the commentaries at the beginning to provide further inspiration. After your third cycle (i.e.: after 27 days of doing the program), you may not feel the same need to use the commentaries before beginning with Step One. At that point, just use your intuition to feel what is appropriate.

Gradual Change through Regular Practice

The 40-day program is based on the application of principles that have proven to be effective in a variety of traditions of spiritual healing. Inspite of being effective, however, their efficacy is not instantaneous. Instant miracles are always a possibility but statistically unlikely and should not be expected. Thus you'll need to give the principles enough time and attention in order to work.

To the degree that you have doubt about your ability to receive their efficacy, is the same degree of effort you will need to put in the program. In other words, you'll need to give this time and attention to yourself so that, with the support of the 40-day program, you are in a position to allow them to work. You will need to first notice the hidden factors in your life that cause a state of imbalance or even illness, then progress to feeling your way through them until they dissipate and eventually, without forcing things unnaturally, implement some healthy changes in your habits and attitudes.

Most likely, this will not happen overnight. It took many years of conditioning and habitual repetition to bring about your present situation. Consequently, it will take some time to reverse this selfsame conditioning, your attitudes and habits. Although awareness always works instantaneously, awareness may take a while to trickle down through body/mind to bring about mental and emotional as well as physical changes. At the same time it is important that you don't program yourself that change always needs a long time to take effect. In some cases it happens surprisingly fast. In other words, don't expect miracles, but be open to receiving them when they happen – as sometimes they do very quickly.

This program involves focusing on nine themes. You work with one theme each day, thus one full cycle takes nine days to complete. Nine days are not a very long time. The ideal route is to complete the program four times in succession without a break over thirty-six days and then follow the instructions for the final four days, making it a total of forty days. This is also the format that we suggest.

40 is a significant number in many of the world's spiritual traditions. There seems to be a consensus among the ancients that it takes forty days of repetition of a spiritual practice, to experience a shift in consciousness. For example, the traditional Sufi retreat lasts forty days. Jesus was in the desert for 40 days. Moses was on the mountain for 40 days. In South India, there is a special spiritual retreat for Hindus, which lasts for forty days.

After the four cycles plus the four extra days are completed, it is a good idea to suspend the continuation of the program and assess your situation. Ask yourself: "How do I feel now?" "What have I learned?", "What are the changes that have manifested?", "Are there other changes that still need to happen?", "Have I participated fully?", "Is there more for me to learn through this program?". If yes, you can take it up again at a later time, or if you feel like it, start again after only one week of suspension. Do whatever suits you, and what your inner voice tells you to do.

When we first started putting this book and program together, we did so because we were inspired by the many positive responses from readers of the

42-day Abundance Program in Paula's *Abundance through Reiki*. Even though *Abundance through Reiki* has been out for over six years, people still keep writing about their experiences and how doing the 42-day program has helped them grow and change their entire outlook on life. The end result is that they are able to feel their feelings fully, without losing their equilibrium. A new sense of equanimity is the most talked about benefit.

In fact, one of Paula's students, now a successful seminar leader in his own right, has gone through the 42-day abundance program many times, once for as long as 84 days in a row. It has been the central focus of his spiritual practice and the main source of inspiration for his own work with his clients and students. For him it was not so much a quick-fix tool but an inspiration to explore the non-dual nature of reality. Through this he found both deep and lasting satisfaction as well as a focus point for his career as a corporate consultant, spiritual mentor and seminar leader. He found natural abundance, self-reliance and a growing sense of fulfillment.

The 40-day program of the 9 Principles to Absolute Wellness was put together with the same intention to provide the reader with a basis for a similarly profound journey of self-discovery, only that this time the focus of the exploration is deep self-healing.

In the course of such explorations, dramatic shifts may sometimes occur while at other times the changes will hardly be noticeable. You may only notice them in retrospect when you reflect on your shift in attitude. Thus it is necessary to pay attention and keep the light of your inner awareness shining. For some, it will be helpful to pick up the program again at a later date, may be even years later, to explore a new set of challenges and the attitude in which they are faced.

There is no end to the depth you can go with this, as the entire process is meant to be open-ended. The secret of the program is not in the program itself. The secret is in you - and in your willingness to re-examine your life with its help. The program can only be a key. You are both the lock and the treasure chest to be opened.

The Key Elements for A Successful 40-Day Program

The tremendous success people have achieved in the 42-Day Abundance Plan, included in Paula's book *Abundance through Reiki* is due to four key factors. These same elements also apply to the 40-Day Program. Although each program has a different emphasis, both are designed to increase awareness, which in itself provides a broad matrix for positive change. For awareness to evolve, unfold, and grow, a certain protocol is necessary. Below are the four key elements that when followed, will ensure a perceptible breakthrough in consciousness. They will enable you to get in touch with yourself in a way you may never have dreamed possible.

DESIRE: The first element necessary to a successful 40-Day Program is *heartfelt desire*. Not the illusory desire of fantasy yearnings, which only takes you down a blind alley. Heartfelt desire liberates you. Heartfelt desire to wake up from your suffering, will ultimately set you free. It is the desire we all have inside, for the Truth that we really are. At times, it manifests as deep longing, which seeps through the cracks of our everyday existence, and creates dissatisfaction when we are not true to ourselves. Instead of ignoring this desire, if we fuel it and stoke it with a strong determination to live our Truth, existence will eventually create the circumstances we need to make that happen. Freedom from physical and mental suffering can only happen with an awakened, free consciousness. To receive it, you have to focus on it with such an enthusiasm and intensity, that all other distractions are burned in the fire of this sacred yearning. Without this strong desire, liberation is next to impossible. Therefore, become aware of your desire. Tend it well, and it will reward you a hundred-fold.

COMMITMENT: To receive the desired results of the 40-Day Program, a strong commitment to follow through, is necessary. When we dedicatedly commit to something, we effectively remove all doubt and ambiguity. The attitude "I'll try this" will get you nowhere. Hidden in the word "try" is the ego's excuse for sabotaging any action you fail to follow through on, all the way. The phrase, "well, at least, I tried" is a meek excuse for not putting all your energy behind something. So, beware of the word "try". Because this program is about helping you learn to feel and thus release the resistance of the ego, a lot of your resistance will naturally come up. If you are not willing to make a very clear commitment right from the start to participate fully, by *feeling* fully, and not just thinking about the various themes that are given, do not expect any real results. Your conditioning is what is keeping you in your suffering, and it has a vested interest in maintaining the status quo. Only a strong commitment right from the start and fostered every day, will allow you to break through the patterns, which have led to your dissatisfaction or disease.

CONSISTENCY: The number of days in this program is the exact same number it takes, while doing an awareness practice on a daily basis, to experience a shift in consciousness. It is also necessary to follow through every day for all 40 days without interruption, to experience a marked change regarding your present challenge, or regarding the attitude you have toward it. It is crucial that you finish the program in one continuous flow and not miss one day! If you miss even one day, results will be compromised, as the momentum necessary to break the force of habit and conditioning, will be interrupted. If for any reason, you forget one day, simply start over from the beginning, even if you miss day 38. Through your forgetfulness, Consciousness lets you know that you need to work with the program a little longer at this time. The conditioning that is currently controlling you has taken many years and even lifetimes to develop. It is unrealistic to expect it to shift without a consistent and disciplined effort. There is a need in this program to consistently focus on and feel whatever theme is pinpointed. The program is designed to help foster a natural vigilance in all matters and all circumstances, as they arise. The secret is, you must first instigate this consistent vigilance yourself, by following through every day for only 40 days.

DETACHMENT: There is a great irony in the fact that, in order to glean real benefits from this program, it is essential that you detach yourself from the results. In Paula's Reiki classes, she always explains how important it is for a healer to not approach a patient with any attachment to a certain outcome. It is one thing to wish the patient well and confidently encourage them that healing is possible. It is another to have an attachment to the actual results. It only provokes further unconscious resistance from the patient. When we are attached to any idea, a certain resistance will result. Attachment has a grasping energy about it. It infers a lack of total trust in the universe. Instead of getting what we want, we end up pushing it away.

There is also a certain paradox involved in detachment. For example, in regard to this program, you can be very specific about the end result you are seeking. On the other hand it is best to be open and not particular about how exactly this result should manifest. In other words, you want to avoid any clinging notions about how greater health and well-being will manifest, in regard to the particular "package" it will come in. Instead, fully trusting in the universe, you assume an open attitude that it will provide you with your highest and best good. In other words, you are open to the end result possibly going beyond your own expectations.

The importance about being clear about your intention, is that decisive clarity puts out a certain energy field that attracts to it, all the various elements we need, to manifest this selfsame intention. When such intention is complemented with detachment, the trust that it implies ensures that you receive what you have intended. The trust inherent in detachment also ensures that you are open to receiving. Thus people who are clear about what they want, yet are not attached to it manifesting in a certain way, are finally able to receive their heartfelt desires.

Each day, as you begin this program and later as you go about your life, consider these four keys as helpmates on the path. Heartfelt desire, dedicated commitment, consistent devotion and clear detachment all work together to ensure satisfying results in all of your endeavors.

Chapter 11

The 40-Day Program

Questioning and being aware: these are the most precious teachers. They dwell in the heart of every human being, who begins to awaken to the waste and danger of an unexamined life.

— *Tarthang Tulku*

You are about to embark on a journey of discovery into the outer appearance and inner source of your imbalance or ailment. However, it is *not* the *direct* aim or goal of this journey of discovery to get rid of your imbalance or ailment. Such a motivation is inherently resistant and only creates persistence of the problem. Yes, the wish to be free of whatever is troubling you, is the motivation to get you started. The desired release from your discomfort will also very often be the *indirect* outcome of this endeavor.

However, it is crucial for you to remember that the immediate goal is to become more aware of yourself and the dynamics of your life. The result will be that you will become more intimately acquainted with yourself and with who you truly are. This deeply intimate experience of who you are, will eventually contribute to physical and psychological healing. It may not cure a fatal disease, however it will help lift the burden and transcend the identification we always have with our suffering.

This in itself is one of the most healing experiences that we can grant ourselves: the direct knowledge that we are *not* our suffering, even if we suffer. Suffering is there, no doubt. It happens. It does indeed afflict us and flow through us. If we are willing to pay attention, it may even become our teacher and reveal things about us that we need to understand and integrate.

But we need to understand also that we are not this suffering. It is not our essence. It is not who we are. As it is we who perceive the suffering, we are the master, and suffering only the messenger of an imbalance in need of correction.

In essence, we are Consciousness. Consciousness is totally open, non-resistant and non-material, yet can accommodate the material. It is able to reflect any shape or form, play out any drama that needs to unfold according to the dictates of karma. Due to its innate freedom of defining qualities, Consciousness can take on any disguise needed to provide for whatever is asked for in the moment. We can best compare Consciousness to a crystal stone. When you put a crystal on a colored surface, its untinted nature is concealed as it takes on the color of its backdrop. However for the pristine clarity of the crystal to become obvious, you only need to remove the crystal from the surface. Then you can see its clarity.

In the following 40-Day Program, we explore, notice and feel into all of the manifestations of Consciousness that are troubling us because, as of now, due to the trouble itself, it is obvious that consciousness is out of synchronization with reality. Something, even though it is unintentional, has not been attended to. Somewhere we have not allowed our feelings to surface.

Only through our imbalance or ailment are we forced to finally confront them. This is the gift of any imbalance or ailment. It points out to us that we have fallen out of our original perfection and perfect wellness, while at the same time it calls us to return to this selfsame state on a deeper level of integration; with a thorough understanding and greater compassion for ourselves and all beings.

In other words, in the course of the 40-Day Program, you are guided to feel through the various manifestations of Consciousness, to uncover its pristine luminosity - your light of awareness. Such awareness has a profound healing power and can help us recognize the depth of all of existence.

Guidelines for a Successful Approach to Self-Inquiry

To successfully complete the 40-Day Program, a simple willingness to get up 30 minutes earlier each day for 40 days is necessary. In addition, what is needed, is the heartfelt desire to directly feel and explore the dynamics that shape your present situation. When you commit to follow through with all of the guidelines, you effectively remove any sense of ambiguity or doubt, which could otherwise distract you from a successful completion of the program. A commitment to follow through will help focus the cultivation of the primary subtle energy, which is so essential for drawing to you all the circumstances you will need for the best results. The energy behind a strong commitment will also help you see clearly what needs to be cultivated in your present situation, and what you can effectively let go of. Ultimately, it dissolves doubt and confusion and supports you with the inner strength to gain real benefit. Begin the 40-Day Program only when you can carry through with the following guidelines.

1. Start the 40-Day Program only when you have determined that it is your Heart's desire to do so, and that you are absolutely committed to following through all the way.

2. You have no doubt that you will do the program every day for 40 consecutive days.

3. You are also ready to make the commitment to yourself that, should you forget to practice one day, you will immediately start again with Day 1 until you have completed the full 40-Day Program in one continuous flow.

4. You agree to spend at least 30 minutes each day for 40 days on the program. You will spend approximately 15 minutes on the expansion process and self-inquiry in Step 2, and the other 15 minutes on the other 4 Steps combined.

5. You agree to always do all 5 Steps. Not for one day will you leave any element of the program out, as there is a certain synergy to them.

6. You agree to not share your process with anyone prematurely. In other words, first complete the program and then talk about it, if at all. People who are not involved in the same process may think that what you are doing is funny and distract you from your purpose. However, if you are doing the program in the framework of a support group, you may share your experiences in your group meetings. In this case mutual shar-

ing will support your efforts and help clarify the process you are undergoing.

7. Relax! Be very focused in your process, but also very relaxed. In this program you implant the habit of feeling and understanding yourself from the inside, which later will give you an increased sense of self-reliance and quiet confidence. The more you keep focused in a relaxed manner, the easier results can manifest of their own accord.

You understand that these suggestions are given by Consciousness to support and help you in your journey of self-discovery. As such you are taking them on voluntarily and of your own free will as guidelines for your practice of the 40-Day Program.

Days 1, 10, 19, & 28

The Principle of Self Respect/Commentary:

"Slow down! Allow yourself to feel the message this imbalance or illness is conveying."

The entire success of the program is built on the premise that by learning to feel ourselves, we can become totally aware of and then transcend the events that happen to us. Feeling what is happening in the moment is the golden key. Through feeling, we get a first real and direct sense of what is actually troubling us. Later we may also gain an insight into the message this imbalance or illness is conveying, which is important for determining how to act.

The insight into the message of slowing down is indeed the basis for all the actions that follow, which can remove the imbalance or illness. If we race at breakneck speed through each day and all of the circumstances that occur, we will never have the opportunity to experience the true depth which available to us. Therefore, to really feel what is going on inside and around us, we need to slow down. We need to shift to a gentler pace to be in a position to be aware and notice.

When we are racing down the highway, we don't notice the landscape. We fail to really take in the rivers, the mountains and the shifting clouds. When we rush through our days, we even forget to notice the simple fact that we are actually alive. We may simply shut down and stop feeling altogether. This incessant rushing about greatly compounds any challenges that arise in life. It is what turns them into problems. Really feel the genuine wisdom in slowing down.

The Principle of Self Respect/Step 1

Find a comfortable position in your favorite place and give yourself a few moments to become quiet. Breathe naturally, yet deeply and let your entire body/mind relax. Take a deep sigh of relief, allowing the sound Aahhh... to reverberate from your belly and directly experience how you cast off your burden. Do this as many times as you need to. If your thoughts are active, allow them to be there. Simply observe them intently as they pass through. Feel yourself relax, allowing any tight muscles to simply let go. Although completely relaxed, stay alert and attentive, noticing any physical sensations as well as thoughts going through the mind ..... noticing all sensations and thoughts, but not getting hooked on them. Focus now, on the subject you wish to explore more deeply:

The Principle of Self-Respect/Step 2

Now that you are relaxed, you can begin to reflect from Heart about your present situation. Most often, when we become disturbed, we resort to "trying to figure out a solution" with a mind that is also disturbed. This desperate type of approach does not yield the best solutions. Instead, when we consciously choose to slow down, by either simply slowing down the breath, breathing deeply and/or stopping whatever we are doing and sitting for a moment, to just feel and direct our attention inward, we create space for a solution to bubble up.

The mind will slow down, when we put all of our focus, all of our attention on it and allow it to chatter freely. When you focus and invite the thoughts to come, they magically disappear (as long as you are clearly not trying to make them go away). When the mind begins to move slowly, you begin to take many things in all at once and actually integrate them – including your feelings. It is like being in the middle of a car accident when time seems to slow down while the car is rolling over and over very quickly. It all happens in a couple of seconds, yet it seems like minutes as everything unfolds in slow motion.

It is best not to wait for an accident or a crisis to evoke such alertness. You can do that now and use your focus to begin assessing your situation. Hold one hand over your heart and the other over your belly. Begin to breathe slowly and deeply so that both hands are pushed out each time you inhale. Continue for five minutes. Now with both hands over your heart, allow yourself to feel whatever the heart wants to communicate.

Keep your attention on your heart and let it speak. The response may come out as a specific thought, or a feeling may arise. Whatever happens, continue to breathe slowly and allow it to be.

Keeping this slow pace, contemplate your present condition. If you are unhappy, unbalanced or dissatisfied, allow yourself to feel what this unhappiness, dissatisfaction or emotional imbalance is trying to convey. If you are sick or even gravely ill, explore with an open heart the feeling or message your illness may carry. Give yourself ample time for this exploration, and do not allow yourself to be pulled into a frantic mental search for the root cause. There may be many different interconnected causes. Simply intend that they reveal themselves in their own time, if needed. Remain open and receptive, and let all the different insights or feelings come up of their own accord. Slowly examining their message, stay focused on this process until you feel that it is complete for the time being.

The Principle of Self Respect/Step 3

Read the following statement out loud three consecutive times, giving a voice to your heart and true nature, strong and filled with the conviction of what is so:

*For the sake of my own well-being, that of my loved ones
    and all of creation,*

From now until Awareness is recognized as all-pervasive,

I give myself always, all the time and space I need

To really listen to myself

*And to feel the message my present state of being
    Is conveying to me;*

The lesson it urges me to learn.

I open myself to health and wholeness,

At one with the ever-present truth of my own nature.

*Fully felt, may this truth now radiate outward
    touching and*

Inspiring all beings to feel their own deepest truth,

*Bestowing happiness and health and true equanimity
    and relieving suffering everywhere.*

The Principle of Self Respect/Step 4

Sit quietly for a few moments and absorb the impact of your own exploration as well as the words that you have just read out loud three times. Feel your own truth radiating throughout, gently, patiently and gradually repatterning your body/mind into a matrix of health and wholesomeness.

The Principle of Self Respect/Step 5

Now take five to ten minutes to write your observations for the day in the special diary that you have acquired for the 40-Day Program to Absolute Wellness.

Days 2, 11, 20 & 29

The Principle of Awareness/Commentary:
"Notice what you are resisting in your life."

When we slow down and start to feel, we begin to get in touch with all of the perceptions and feelings that we usually avoid. We notice what we normally resist. Although uncomfortable at first, this is actually a major step in the right direction. The path to balance and health always requires total honesty. Balance and health cannot exist side by side with denial. It simply isn't possible.

We all know the saying that "what you resist persists". In the second theme, we learn to apply the wisdom of this common insight to our advantage. We do this by focusing the full light of our awareness on whatever we are resisting or whatever we have pretended not to notice because of the pain it evokes. We then discover how dropping our resistance allows the pain to flow through quietly.

Before anything can change for the better, it is necessary to take stock of our situation. This is simply a matter of taking a realistic assessment of the present circumstances we find ourselves in. A doctor could not help his or her patients if he or she refused to be realistic regarding the state of the patients' health. In the same way, it is impossible to come out of what is troubling and irritating us, to the point of making us sick, if we opt out and feign ignorance and pretend not to notice what is actually happening.

We simply need to be realistic, in order to find ways to become balanced and well. It is therefore essential to notice what is happening, without labeling it "bad" or on the other hand, by outrightly ignoring certain crucial elements.

The Principle of Awareness/Step 1

Find a comfortable position, in your favorite place and give yourself a few moments to become quiet. Breathe naturally, yet deeply and let your entire body/mind relax. Take a deep sigh of relief, allowing the sound Aahhh... to reverberate from your belly and directly experience how you cast off your burden. Do this as many times as you need to. If your thoughts are active, allow them to be there. Simply observe them intently as they pass through. Feel yourself relax, allowing any tight muscles to simply let go. Although completely relaxed, stay alert and attentive, noticing any physical sensations as well as thoughts going through the mind,... noticing all sensations and thoughts, but not getting hooked on them. Focus now, on the subject you wish to explore more deeply.

The Principle of Awareness/Step 2

Once again slow down your breathing and take three especially deep breaths to begin. Place at least one of your hands over your heart to anchor your attention there and focus on what you are resisting in your life. Drawing on your insights from yesterday's session, notice if you are resisting a particular person or condition in your life that seems to be overwhelming.

Allow yourself to first notice all of your resistance to that person or condition. Also notice, if you have some of the same traits, which disturb you so much in another. Perhaps, they are traits that you yourself don't often play out, yet they nonetheless exist. Feel if your anger at another or at some situation is really anger at yourself.

If you are resisting long buried anger or even hatred, give yourself permission to fully feel this anger and hatred now. All emotions, like thoughts, are simply manifestations of a certain energy frequency, as is everything in the universe. Every emotion or thought has a limited energy field. When we concentrate *all* of our attention on a thought or emotion (without trying to make it go away), it soon dissipates.

So, focus now on any irritation you are feeling, and with your eyes closed, imagine the energy field of this irritation expanding in all directions, ever outward all around you. Focus and feel and/or visualize the energy continually expanding. If a memory, thought, or bodily sensation comes up, include these in the process, and keep expanding. If tears come, let them fall and bring your attention back to the energy expanding. The exercise is complete, when you reach the outermost limits, and there is simply nothing left to expand. You'll know you are complete because you will feel very clear. If you get sleepy during the expansion process, this is only resistance to feeling. Include even the sleepiness, and expand it as part of the process. Continue to observe the energy expanding until it is complete.

The entire process is totally effortless. If you have any difficulty, it is because you are trying too hard. Simply *stop trying* and instead *observe* it happening.

If that you are resisting a lot of grief allow yourself to clearly feel and acknowledge it. Focus on it and expand it too, until it dissipates. Be willing and ready now, to openly explore all of your resistance, remembering that emotional disturbances and physical illnesses are psychosomatic and karmic. This exercise is to be done with your heart, not your head. As you feel and expand your primary resistances, be sure that you keep your awareness on your heart. Stay focused on the process of expanding your resistance until you have a sense that you are complete for the time being.

The Principle of Awareness/Step 3

Read the following statement out loud three consecutive times, giving voice from the heart of your true nature, strong and filled with the conviction of what is so:

For the sake of my own well-being, that of my loved ones
    And all of creation,

From now until Awareness is recognized as all-pervasive,

I acknowledge my resistance,

I open all my senses to notice the grief that I've held
    onto;
    The long forgotten hurt that I still carry;
    The grudges that I bear;

Any anger that seethes repressed in each and every cell,
    I now feel and release.

Any aversion or hatred that lie hidden;

The many unfulfilled desires that drive me to distraction,
    I now feel and let go of.

The illusions that I have cherished although I know them
   to be fleeting, I let go of.

I drop the fetters of self-deception and denial, and by
   clearly noticing
   What has disturbed me all along,

I open to deeper understanding of the causes of my
   misfortune.

Once noticed, may these insights then radiate outward,
   touching and

Inspiring all beings to acknowledge their own desire and
   resistance.

May the liberation from self deception and denial prevail,

Thus bestowing happiness and health and true
   equanimity
   And relieving suffering everywhere.

The Principle of Awareness/Step 4

Sit quietly for a few moments and absorb the impact of your own exploration as well as the words that you have just read out loud three times. Feel your own truth radiating throughout, gently, patiently and gradually repatterning your body/mind into a matrix of health and wholesomeness.

The Principle of Awareness/Step 5

Now, take five to ten minutes to write your observations for the day in a special diary that you have acquired for the 40-Day Program to Absolute Wellness.

Days 3, 12, 21 & 30

The Principle of Letting Go/Commentary:
"Allow yourself to feel this resistance."

This step may seem almost identical with the previous injunction. However there is a subtle difference. It goes one step further, from noticing and beginning to feel what we resist, to fully feeling the resistance itself, and only then returning to the actual theme of resistance, finally completing any residual feelings, which are left. When we notice something, we look at it from the outside with our mind and effectively externalize it. When we feel something, we feel it very much from the inside, reverberating through our body/mind. Today you will go to a greater depth with this process.

With the second theme you stand at the shore, so to speak, and watch the waves of memories and emotions arise and then begin to touch on the feelings. With the third theme you dive into the water and feel these waves and explore what is inside of them.

The Principle of Letting Go/Step 1

Find a comfortable position, in your favorite place and give yourself a few moments to become quiet. Breathe naturally, yet deeply and let your entire body/mind relax. Take a deep sigh of relief, allowing the sound Aahhh... to reverberate from your belly and directly experience how you cast off your burden. Do this as many times as you need to. If your thoughts are active, allow them to be there. Simply observe them intently as they pass through. Feel yourself relax, allowing any tight muscles to simply let go. Although completely relaxed, stay alert and attentive, noticing any physical sensations as well as thoughts going through the mind,... noticing all sensations and thoughts, but not getting hooked on them. Focus now, on the subject you wish to explore more deeply.

The Principle of Letting Go/Step 2

Now that you are relaxed, begin again with the theme of resistance you worked on yesterday. For issues that provoked a lot of resistance you may need to repeat the expansion process three times. The issues that make you fall asleep during the exercise, are "the closest to home". If you find yourself growing fatigued stand up and continue the process.

Yesterday we focused on expanding resistance. Continue that process until you feel clearer and lighter. Then shift the focus to the actual theme you are resisting (be it a person or a circumstance), and imagine it expanding. In other words, on a very practical level, whenever you feel angry or resistant toward something, sharpen your focus and expand the anger or resistance first. Then observe the energy expand in regard to the actual circumstance. If you succeeded yesterday in neutralizing your resistance (when you felt clear or "light" at the end of the process), today finish expanding any energy or "juice" you are still holding regarding the actual circumstance. If you noticed an inability to expand something yesterday, simply observe yourself expanding "your inability to expand". Remember, the expansion of the energy is effortless – simply observe it while feeling it happening.

Now, with the intention to notice whatever is there, feel into what you are still strongly in resistance to. Your unconscious reactive pattern for dealing with resistance is most likely to avoid what you resist. This reaction, although understandable, is self- defeating, as we all know that what we resist, persists. Therefore, instead of continuing to avoid what you resist, you now want to feel it fully.

Just remember what you noticed yesterday, especially what feels incomplete, and today dive into it and feel it fully. Don't hold back. Really feel what you resent or are resisting is doing to you. Fully feel how it is effecting you, and also feel and expand all the related feelings that are connected with this person or issue that you resist.

The Principle of Letting Go/Step 3

Read the following statement out loud three consecutive times, giving a voice to your heart and true nature, strong and filled with the conviction of what is so:

For the sake of my own well-being, that of my loved-ones
    And all of Creation,
From now until Awareness is recognized as all-pervasive,
I feel fully what pains me, and what I strongly resist.
I allow intrinsic awareness to take charge so that I feel
    And let go of the long forgotten hurt that I still carry
    And any resentment that I hold

I willingly feel the anger that seethes repressed in eac **ı**
    and every cell;
    Any aversion or hatred that I have unknowlingly hold
    on to.

I also feel my unfulfilled desires and the illusions that I
    cherish
    Although I know them to be fleeting.

I now drop all the fig leaves of self-deception and self-
    denial
    And by fully feeling

What has disturbed me all along,

I open to letting go of the causes of my misfortune.

Now felt and let go of, may my release radiate outward

Inspiring all beings to also feel their own resistance
    And unfulfilled desires.

May genuine feelings permeate the world,

Thus bestowing happiness, health and equanimity,
    And relieving suffering everywhere.

The Principle of Letting Go/Step 4

Sit quietly for a few moments and absorb the impact of your exploration as well as the words that you just read out loud three times. Feel your own truth radiating throughout, gently, patiently and gradually repatterning your body/mind into a matrix of health and wholesomeness.

The Principle of Letting Go/Step 5

Finally take five to ten minutes to write your observations for the day in the special diary that you have acquired for the 40-Day Program to Absolute Wellness.

Days 4, 13, 22 & 31

The Principle of Courage/Commentary:
"Address whatever fear is there, and feel it."

So far you have accomplished the following steps: You have slowed down. You have also determined what you don't want to continue to have in your life by noticing what you resist. Finally, you have allowed yourself to feel the resistance you have to a certain issue in your life whose influence you wish to curtail. These three steps should by now have made you acutely aware of the challenge you are now prepared to deal with.

Feeling your resistance inevitably brings up fear. You need to address this fear now, especially if your condition is serious. You need to feel it. Many of us may have memories from childhood when we dealt with fear by whistling in the dark, in order to keep our fear at arm's length. As children, very few of us had mentors to teach us how to deal with fear. Now, as adults we have the opportunity.

We can actually allow ourselves to feel our fear fully. Repressing it won't make it go away. In fact, there is no trick, which will ever make it disappear. The only way out of it, is through it. Even then, some fear will remain, but it will no longer cloud our perception or compromise our decisions. Instead of being oppressive, it will become our wise counselor. It will caution us to avoid people, things and circumstances that can potentially harm us. There will always be some element of fear, as long as we are prone to even the slightest residue of identification with anything that is impermanent. And everything is impermanent except pure Awareness.

However, fear that cautions us and guides us to be watchful, is actually healthy and helpful. In order to turn our unconscious and blinding fears into allies on the path to greater health and wholesomeness all we have to do, is address them and feel them fully. Noticing our fear in every minute aspect and detail and feeling it without holding back, provides for a special kind of alchemy, which transforms the emotion of fear into the knowledge of the appropriate path that will help you recognize your freedom.

The Principle of Courage/Step 1

Find a comfortable position, in your favorite place and give yourself a few moments to become quiet. Breathe naturally, yet deeply and let your entire body/mind relax. Take a deep sigh of relief, allowing the sound Aahhh... to reverberate from your belly and directly experience how you cast off your burden. Do this as many times as you need to. If your thoughts are active, allow them to be there. Simply observe them intently as they pass through. Feel yourself relax, allowing any tight muscles to simply let go. Although completely relaxed, stay alert and attentive, noticing any physical sensations as well as thoughts going through the mind,... noticing all sensations and thoughts, but not getting hooked on them. Focus now, on the subject you wish to explore more deeply.

The Principle of Courage/Step 2

Chances are, in the previous two sessions, you began to feel the fear underlying all resistance. Two major fears we all carry, are the fear of rejection (from our need for approval) and the fear of losing our security. These two are always with us and need to be addressed.

If you want to maintain or regain your emotional balance and physical health, you need to address your fear directly. You can no longer sweep it under the carpet and pretend that it doesn't exist. As long as we are identified with the body/mind we will always suffer from fear. Because the body is impermanent (and we know it), we fear its loss. This is the primary fear of ego. All others are subservient to this one fear, yet each one needs to be felt.

How is this accomplished? Exactly in the same way as in the previous two steps where you expanded the major blocks of resistance that hold you in bondage, imbalance and disease: By noticing your fear and then feeling it fully and expanding it.

First take stock of the particular kind of fears that were evoked in the previous two sessions. Make a mental note of them. Then, imagine them very clearly. Dive into them and feel them fully throughout the body. Feel how it feels to be confronted with the energy of this fear. Notice if you feel any particular sensations in the body. If you do, put all your attention on the constricted muscles, the tight stomach and imagine the sensation expanding. Put all your attention on the fear and allow it to expand as if of its own accord, until it dissipates and you feel clear. You are not trying to make the fear disappear, you are simply letting it expand energetically until there is nothing left to expand. You will know it is complete when you feel clear and all fatigue is gone.

When you feel your exploration is complete for the time being, continue with the next step.

The Principle of Courage/Step 3

Read the following statement out loud three consecutive times, giving a voice to your heart and true nature, strong and filled with the conviction of what is so:

For the sake of my own well-being, that of my loved-ones
And all of Creation,

From now until Awareness is recognized as all-pervasive,
I willingly face my fear.

I acknowledge this fear that I've held within me, which
has control led my life and held me back,
Either in a concealed fashion or plain for all to see.

I name my fear, look it in the eye, and say:
It is you, it is Death that I fear.

By thus acknowledging the root of my worries, doubts
and concerns,

I recognize what has sabotaged my efforts and sapped my
strength.

As I face and feel my fear, may this new found freedom

Inspire all beings to face their own fear, the greatest of
which
Is the fear of the annihilation of the imagined separate
self.

May the casting off of the burden of ego
Bestow happiness, health and equanimity
And relieve suffering everywhere.

The Principle of Courage/Step 4

Sit quietly for a few moments and absorb the impact of your exploration as well as the words that you just read out loud three times. Feel your own truth radiating throughout, gently, patiently and gradually repatterning your body/mind into a matrix of health and wholesomeness.

The Principle of Courage/Step 5

Finally take five to ten minutes to write your observations for the day in the special diary that you have acquired for the 40-Day Program to Absolute Wellness

Days 5, 14, 23 & 32

The Principle of Compassion/Commentary:
"Forgive yourself or another."

Very often we become psychologicaliy unbalanced or even physically ill because we have not forgiven ourselves or another human being for some past event. All genuine spiritual traditions agree that Consciousness is the ultimate "judge" of right or wrong because in Consciousness "right" or "wrong" actually do not exist, only ignorance does. From this it logically follows that there is no external power or God weighing our sins and condemning us for what we have done wrong, or what we believe we have done wrong.

However, Consciousness effortlessly corrects all imbalances. Whatever suffering we are experiencing now, is the consequence of a hurtful action that happened in the past. The way out of suffering is always to acknowledge its cause by feeling its effect (which incidentally, is the purpose of this entire 40-day program). It is not even necessary to know the original cause.

Therefore, we need to acknowledge the facts. We can feel our remorse and apologize wholeheartedly. As soon as this is done, we need to forgive ourselves.

Genuine remorse is very helpful and empowering, for it fosters a sense of responsibility.

On the other hand, feelings of guilt are neither curative, nor are they empowering. Feelings of guilt never compensate for past actions; they only attract them back more powerfully. Rather than being helpful, feeling guilty is on the contrary destructive and freezes us in a state of unwholesomeness and possibly disease. Feeling guilty robs us of our willpower to act positively because these feelings seduce us to wallow in them, and create a resulting sense of helplessness. Ultimately, the resentment they create causes us to lash out and start the whole cycle over again.

The correct medicine for the senseless mind-games of the merry-go-round of guilt and sin (which is sadly enough very often encouraged and even cultivated by organized religion) are, again, the feelings of genuine remorse and forgiveness. Once we have allowed ourselves to feel genuine remorse and forgiven ourselves and others for the past, we automatically shoulder the responsibility for whatever has occurred. This sense of responsibility releases us from being stuck in memory. We are then naturally free to take appropriate action in every moment.

The Principle of Compassion/Step 1

Find a comfortable position, in your favorite place and give yourself a few moments to become quiet. Breathe naturally, yet deeply and let your entire body/mind relax. Take a deep sigh of relief, allowing the sound Aahhh... to reverberate from your belly and directly experience how you cast off your burden. Do this as many times as you need to. If your thoughts are active, allow them to be there. Simply observe them intently as they pass through. Feel yourself relax, allowing any tight muscles to simply let go. Although completely relaxed, stay alert and attentive, noticing any physical sensations as well as thoughts going through the mind,... noticing all sensations and thoughts, but not getting hooked on them. Focus now, on the subject you wish to explore more deeply:

The Principle of Compassion/Step 2

There is a strong connection between the amount of guilt you carry around with you, either consciously or unconsciously, and the severity of your emotional imbalance or physical illness. Like fear, guilt will exercise a tight control over your life. Guilt is actually a very insidious feeling, as it is often implanted in you to further someone else's agenda. Guilt is neither clean nor honest, it is a perverted form of remorse. Genuine remorse is something you feel from the bottom of your heart for a wrong that you have committed either knowingly or unknowingly, either in this lifetime or in a previous incarnation.

If you are aware that you have wronged someone, feel the remorse that will naturally arises, apologize sincerely and then get on with your life. Don't allow anyone to burden you with guilt so that they can control you. Likewise, if you feel that someone else has wronged you, speak out, stand up for yourself and understand that they have only acted out of ignorance. Even if they harmed and hurt you intentionally, this is just an expression of their basic ignorance. They obviously have not recognized the fact that by harming and hurting you, they are ultimately hurting themselves much more than they could ever harm you.

Therefore, feel deeply into whatever wrong you have committed, or that has been done to you. Imagine them very clearly, and all the pain that this situation has created. Expand the feelings that come up until they dissipate. Then forgive yourself and others, for the wrong and for the pain, and effectively let go of any remaining sense of guilt that you are carrying, connected to this wrong. Allow yourself to be healed by forgiveness. It is especially helpful in today's session to expand any guilt or shame that you are carrying until it dissipates. If you are still harboring resentment toward another, expand these feelings also until they dissipate.

Continue with your exploration until you have the sense that you are complete for the day.

The Principle of Compassion/Step 3

Read the following statement out loud three consecutive times, giving a voice to your heart and true nature, strong and filled with the conviction of what is so:

For the sake of my own well-being and that of
    my loved ones
    And all of Creation,

From now until Awareness is recognized as all-pervasive,

I forgive myself for what I feel ashamed of
    And what I have judged as hurtful by another.

Feeling a genuine and deep sense of remorse,
    I forgive myself
    And let go of what needs to be forgiven,

As much as I forgive others for the acts of cruelty
  I believe
  They have committed.

Knowing that all wrongs committed in this world

Are due to the basic ignorance of the mistaken notion of
  self and others
  I cannot but forgive all those trapped
  In this net of ignorance, including myself.

Now complete, let forgiveness radiate outward,

Inspiring all beings to forgive themselves and others.

May the liberating joy of forgiveness permeate the world,

Thus bestowing happiness and health
  And relieving suffering everywhere.

The Principle of Compassion/Step 4

Sit quietly for a few moments and absorb the impact of your exploration as well as the words that you just read out loud three times. Feel your own truth radiating throughout, gently, patiently and gradually repatterning your body/mind into a matrix of health and wholesomeness.

The Principle of Compassion/Step 5

Finally take five to ten minutes to write your observations for the day in the special diary that you have acquired for the 40-Day Program to Absolute Wellness

Days 6, 15, 24 & 33

The Principle of Responsibility/
Commentary:

"Take appropriate action."

As long as we are unconscious and identified with the body and its concomitant mind, we have no real choice in our acions. Rather than limiting and destructive, however, action can also be liberating.

This depends on the motivation and intention with which the action is carried out, and it also depends on the knowledge we have at our disposal when we act. This is why taking appropriate action comes up only now, as theme 6 of the program, and not earlier. Before we are in a position to take appropriate action, we need to thoroughly assess our situation, which was achieved by contemplation on the previous five themes.

Further research may be in order now, if you are dealing with a challenging health problem. A variety of natural healing methods are available, which support the immune system and can gently ease you out any imbalance, rather than attacking the body to kill the disease – an approach that often kills the body as well.

The Principle of Responsibility/Step 1

Find a comfortable position, in your favorite place and give yourself a few moments to become quiet.

Breathe naturally, yet deeply and let your entire body / mind relax. Take a deep sigh of relief, allowing the sound Aahhh... to reverberate from your belly and directly experience how you cast off your burden. Do this as many times as you need to. If your thoughts are active, allow them to be there. Simply observe them intently as they pass through. Feel yourself relax, allowing any tight muscles to simply let go. Although completely relaxed, stay alert and attentive, noticing any physical sensations as well as thoughts going through the mind,... noticing all sensations and thoughts, but not getting hooked on them. Focus now, on the subject you wish to explore more deeply.

The Principle of Responsibility/Step 2

All nine themes are equally important. Yet, to take appropriate action is pivotal. It is the lynchpin on which everything else hinges. Introspection will make things clearer. Feeling your resistance and desire fully, without trying to make it go away, will undoubtedly dissolve them, thus putting you in a position to act. However, if you don't back your insights up with action, especially in the case of illness and severe psychological imbalance, you will not complete what at heart you most want to accomplish. Action is necessary to liberate yourself from the fetters that hold you back. Otherwise you will most likely remain stuck with the present state of your ailment or discomfort.

Now is your chance to quietly contemplate the course of action you need to take. However, there is no need to rush or get frantic. Just sit quietly with the question and ask yourself: "What exactly is it that I need to do, in order to get well or find balance?" Keep an open mind, and allow the answer or answers to come to you. You already know them in your Heart. All that remains to do, is to give them space and time so that they can reveal themselves to you.

Sometimes the answer will be that you need to do a lot more research about your ailment and the various possibilities to tackle it. You may still need some expert opinions, preferably from several distinctly different sources. Sometimes you may need further research as to what these sources might be. There may be a psychological approach, a naturopathic approach, a spiritual approach, and an allopathic or homeopathic approach. In your particular case, you may have to follow more than one approach simultaneously. Thus you may need to have an overall picture of several different possibilities.

The action you need to take may simply involve kicking a bad habit, or an ingrained reactive pattern, which became apparent to you in the previous sessions of the program. Whatever you decide, do something about it. Don't procrastinate, and if your pattern is procrastination (which, of course, is a blatant form of resistance), feel that tendency to procrastinate fully, feel what it does to you and your life, expand it, and then move on.

The main focus here, however, is to keep an open mind and to allow the appropriate course of action to reveal itself. This is the time to let the answers come to you of their own accord, and then visualize yourself taking the action suggested by your own insight and intuition.

Now as you sit quietly, contemplate an appropriate course of action. Then visualize yourself, imagining yourself clearly, following that course of action with full commitment.

The Principle of Responsibility/Step 3

Read the following statement out loud three consecutive times, giving a voice to your heart and true nature, strong and filled with the conviction of what is so:

For the sake of my own well-being, that of my loved ones
And all of Creation,

From now until Awareness is recognized as all-pervasive,

I take action to regain the state of health and balance

That is my own true nature.

I do whatever it takes in my particular case,
To enjoy wellness and harmony in my body and
in my life.

Most of all, I rediscover the love within, that heals all
wounds
And all disease.

I drop the fig-leaf aprons of self-deception

And willingly recognize the habits that lead to sickness
and imbalance.

I open all of my senses to my own natural intelligence

And follow the clear and distinct voice of my
direct insights,

Inspiring all beings to also acknowledge their
inner power

To take matters of their health and sanity in their own
hands.

May the liberation granted by appropriate action prevail,

Thus bestowing happiness and health and true equanim-
  ity
And relieving suffering everywhere.

The Principle of Responsibility/Step 4

Sit quietly for a few moments and absorb the impact of your exploration as well as the words that you just read out loud three times. Feel your own truth radiating throughout, gently, patiently and gradually repatterning your body/mind into a matrix of health and wholesomeness.

The Principle of Responsibility/Step 5

Finally take five to ten minutes to write your observations for the day in the special diary that you have acquired for the 40-Day Program to Absolute Wellness.

Days 7, 16, 25 & 34

The Principle of Love/Commentary:

"Allow yourself to embrace your discomfort or ailment."

Once we start taking action to allow space for a positive change to occur, we have released enough resistance to now be able to embrace our discomfort or ailment. This embracing of what has troubled us, sometimes to the point of seriously threatening our well-being, even our very life, is not the same as meek and passive acceptance or surrendering to some impersonal outer force of fate.

Quite the contrary. It is an expression of our active participation in the shaping of our existence, and reinforces our status as co-creators of our destiny. Furthermore, we usually only embrace someone or something that we have recognized as belonging to us. We don't usually go out in the street and embrace strangers. We embrace those who are near and dear to us. Thus by embracing our ailment or discomfort, we declare it to be our friend and guide.

We attract illness and strife to learn and grow. In the last analysis, they are our own creation. They were called into being by the Consciousness that we ultimately are, to help us become more aware. By embracing illness and strife, we acknowledge this fact.

Through embracing our discomfort or ailment we concede our close involvement with it. We cease making it the enemy, aggressor and threat that needs to be abolished or annihilated. We cease resisting it, and thus "dis-create" its persistence. We dissolve our subject/object relationship with it and come to an even more intimate understanding of its nature. Under these conditions, the going gets easier.

Contracts fully endorsed by all parties involved, are always easier to implement than, for example, hostile take-overs. In this instance it is also good to remember that our bodies and minds have a natural tendency to be healthy and whole, and to heal themselves.

The self-healing power of the body/mind, by far exceeds the power of any medicine or treatment, administered from the outside. Therefore, the body/mind can use the support and encouragement of these inherent self-healing powers much more than any heavy-handed intervention. By embracing our discomfort or ailment and acknowledging the learning process it has provided, we also creatively support the self-healing powers of our bodies and minds.

The Principle of Love/Step 1

Find a comfortable position, in your favorite place and give yourself a few moments to become quiet. Breathe naturally, yet deeply and let your entire body/mind relax. Take a deep sigh of relief, allowing the sound Aahhh... to reverberate from your belly and directly experience how you cast off your burden. Do this as many times as you need to. If your thoughts are active, allow them to be there. Simply observe them intently as they pass through. Feel yourself relax, allowing any tight muscles to simply let go. Although completely relaxed, stay alert and attentive, noticing any physical sensations as well as thoughts going through the mind,... noticing all sensations and thoughts, but not getting hooked on them. Focus now, on the subject you wish to explore more deeply.

The Principle of Love/Step 2

It may seem strange to you, now that you have started to act appropriately, that you are asked to embrace your ailment and discomfort. There may seem to be a contradiction between yesterday's call for action to change your present condition, and to-day's suggestion to embrace whatever ails you.

Actually there is no contradiction. It is simply one of life's many paradoxes. Also, to embrace your ailment or discomfort is not the same as taking it on like an irreversible verdict of fate. To embrace your ailment, specifically means that you allow yourself to learn the lessons that your present condition wishes to convey to you. Remember that, your illness or imbalance is not outside of you or separate from you. It is the creation of the Consciousness that you are, attracted to you to make your body/mind notice where specifically you are out of synchronization with your own wholeness and implicate order.

Your illness or imbalance is not your enemy, it is your ally and guide to greater integration. It may appear to be your adversery, but essentially, if you are willing to see the bigger picture, it is not. If you make use of your ailment or discomfort wisely, you will see that it is there as a stepping stone into greater aware-ness. In one sense, it is your friend, a creation of the Consciousness that you are and designed to help you on your chosen path.

It is also simply a part of you. If you treat it as an intruder or invader that needs to be annihilated, you are bound to treat that particular part of yourself as the enemy that needs to be repelled. You are bound to reject a part of yourself and end up with struggle and strife. If you can embrace your illness or imbalance, however, you openly demonstrate your ability to love unconditionally, and unconditional love is the greatest power throughout the universe. It is also the greatest healer.

Therefore, sit quietly and embrace your ailment for the message it is bringing to you and for the opportunity it affords you, to transform the poison of your self-deception into the wisdom of your own heart. Really listen to your Heart. Whatever message your illness or imbalance carries for you, it will reveal itself as long as you don't try and force the issue with your mind. Just remain quiet and receptive and embrace the issue with arms wide open.

If you still feel resistance to embracing your illness or dissatisfaction, feel this resistance now fully, from your Heart. Expand it until you feel clear and complete.

The Principle of Love/Step 3

Now, read the following statement out loud three consecutive times, giving a voice to your heart and true nature, strong and filled with the conviction of what is so:

For the sake of my own well-being, that of my loved ones
  And all of creation,
From now until Awareness is recognized as all-pervasive,

I openly embrace my ailment and discomfort.

As I have taken action to support my inborn power,
And release disease-producing habits

I now acknowledge my strength to enfold my ailment
and discomfort,

Loving it for the message that it bears and the
opportunity
It affords me to transform the poison of self-deception
Into the wisdom of my Heart.

I drop the fetters of illusory separation
And reconnect with the power of Love,

Inspiring all beings to knowingly embrace what ails them

So that they may also transform the poisons
that plague them
Into the potion of unconditional Love.

May the liberation inherent in embracing
adversity prevail,

Thus bestowing happiness and health and
true equanimity
And relieving suffering everywhere,

The Principle of Love/Step 4

Sit quietly for a few moments and absorb the impact of your exploration as well as the words that you just read out loud three times. Feel your own truth radiating throughout, gently, patiently and gradually repatterning your body/mind into a matrix of health and wholesomeness.

The Principle of Love/Step 5

Finally take five to ten minutes to write your

observations for the day in the special diary that you have acquired for the 40-Day Program to Absolute Wellness.

Days 8, 17, 26 & 35

The Principle of Devotion/Commentary:
"Allow yourself to ask for what you really need."

On the journey to greater balance and/or physical health, certain steps need to be taken so that we can progress successfully and finally come home to our natural state of inborn well-being and equanimity. One important step is to ask for what we need. By asking for what we need, we put out a certain energy, which allows the universe to respond. If we don't ask, the universe cannot so easily respond to what we otherwise hold inside.

Self-healing is something we obviously need. Otherwise, we wouldn't engage in this program. By following the steps of the program, we in fact ask for what we need, both implicitly and explicitly. Sometimes, we need certain assistance from our loved-ones, which they are actually quite happy to give. If we don't ask, it is difficult for them to comply. Too many times we assume that our relatives and friends should know what we need. Often they do, but are afraid to give unless we ask. Ultimately it is up to us to take the risk and ask for what we need, and not assume that our loved ones can read our mind.

Asking for what we need also forces us to abandon our shell of self-protection, which for most has turned into a prison that they dare not step out of. When we ask for something, we make ourselves vulnerable because we have to open our hearts in order to ask. We can, however, call on our courage and overcome what has since childhood been a deeply seated fear of rejection. The vulnerability this brings up, is a prerequisite to self-healing.

It is wise to become childlike again, yet equipped with the experience and knowledge of an adult. Asking for what we need, opens us to our own childlike spirit, essential to all deep forms of healing, be it emotional or even physical. Furthermore, by asking others for what we need, we include them in our quest for wholeness, thus also enlarging the scope of our quest. By reaching out to others we automatically reach more deeply into ourselves.

Asking for what we need is a wholesome practice, which eventually evokes in us an acute awareness of what we truly need. In the field of this awareness, health and well-being can flourish.

The Principle of Devotion/Step 1

Find a comfortable position, in your favorite place and give yourself a few moments to become quiet. Breathe naturally, yet deeply and let your entire body/mind relax. Take a deep sigh of relief, allowing the sound Aahhh... to reverberate from your belly and directly experience how you cast off your burden. Do this as many times as you need to. If your thoughts are active, allow them to be there. Simply observe them intently as they pass through. Feel yourself relax, allowing any tight muscles to simply let go. Although completely relaxed, stay alert and attentive, noticing any physical sensations as well as thoughts going through the mind,... noticing all sensations and thoughts, but not getting hooked on them. Focus now, on the subject you wish to explore more deeply.

The Principle of Devotion/Step 2

In order to fulfill your needs, you first have to know what they are. You have to feel from your heart what it is you really need. Genuine needs are not always identical with the whims and fantasy yearnings implanted in you from the outside. Very often, surface desires actually cover up your real needs. So, what you have been denying yourself can be anything – including greater discipline and focus on your chosen life path.

Your needs are one of the main forces that propelled you into this earthly existence. They are your calling, and if you fulfill them, you will feel a sense of peace. You may not necessarily experience a totally smooth and easy life, but a life well lived. And then, of course, there are the simple gestures from others that we also truly need, like comfort, love and honest communication. These, we also have to ask for.

Take all the time you need to allow yourself to feel what you really need. Explore your need with enthusiasm, diving right into it and feeling it from the inside. Also feel what denying yourself the fulfillment of this need does to you, and the repercussions it has had on the well-being of your body/mind.

Then simply instruct yourself that henceforth you will always ask for what you need. Asking for what you truly need when it comes from the Heart, does not make you an imposing or demanding weakling. On the contrary feeling fully what you need and then asking for it, will elicit the strength and courage to come to the fore that has always been with you, but that you have denied yourself by not acknowledging your true needs.

If you feel any resistance at all to asking for what you need, feel this resistance fully and expand it until you are clear. As you go out into your life today and begin to ask for what you need, always remember that others need you too. By asking them for what you need, you actually fulfill their own need.

The Principle of Devotion/Step 3

Read the following statement out loud three consecutive times, giving a voice to your heart and true nature, strong and filled with the conviction of what is so:

For the sake of my own well-being, that of my loved ones
    And all of Creation,

From now until Awareness is recognized as all-pervasive,

I give myself permission to ask for what I really need:

I allow myself to feel my need fully, from my Heart,
    Knowing all heartfelt needs to be wholesome.

Letting go of all previous denial of my needs,
    fantasy yearnings fall away.

Allowing all that is wholesome to spring forth

From the depths of my own liberated Heart.

I acknowledge my need to see compassion reflected
    in the world
    And in the people that I meet.

Henceforth, in every moment I open to my own need,

Inspiring others to be honest and to voice their own
heartfelt need.

May the power and liberation
Inherent in asking for what I need prevail,

Thus bestowing happiness and health and
true equanimity
And relieving suffering everywhere.

The Principle of Devotion/Step 4

Sit quietly for a few moments and absorb the impact of your exploration as well as the words that you have just read out loud three times. Feel your own truth radiating throughout, gently, patiently and gradually repatterning your body/mind into a matrix of health and wholesomeness.

The Principle of Devotion/Step 5

Finally take five to ten minutes to write your observations for the day in the special diary that you have acquired for the 40-Day Program to Absolute Wellness.

Days 9, 18, 27 & 36

The Principle of Enlightenment/ Commentary:

"Allow yourself to receive fully and whole-heartedly what you truly need."

This is the moment to be expansive and all- "allow-ing" in the truest sense of the word. Many of us are graced with an abundance of blessings, yet we often fail to recognize or accept them when they come our way. Sometimes, asking for what we need, can even turn into a habit, blinding us to the fact that we are already receiving it.

Even in the worst of circumstances, there is the opportunity to use adversity as a tool to waking up. So, in an important way, what may seem like an awful situation, can actually afford us the opportunity to receive the gift of becoming more aware of what is real, and in need of attention.

To receive fully what we need, can mean different things to different people. For some, it means to receive the love and affection that is already given, but remains unnoticed because it does not fit our preconceived notions or expectations. For some it may mean to receive their own power and wisdom and to stop pretending that they are without skills or resources. For others it means to receive the abundance we are already blessed with, but fail to notice because we are programmed to our own detriment, to always want more. For spiritual seekers, it means to deeply recognize their own nature, the fact that as human beings, we essentially have arrived. By nature, we are enlightenment itself. But who is there to notice?

By nature we are also healthy. Disease is not our natural state. It is an aberration of innate equanimity. An appropriate way to enjoy good health, is to focus on and be receptive to our natural state, which will mobilize the self-healing powers inherent in the body/mind and thus take care of many minor imbalances. Whatever it is that we need to learn to receive, large or small, important or seemingly unimportant, the fact is that we do need to be open in order to actually receive.

The Principle of Enlightenment/Step 1

Find a comfortable position, in your favorite place and give yourself a few moments to become quiet. Breathe naturally, yet deeply and let your entire body/mind relax. Take a deep sigh of relief, allowing the sound Aahhh... to reverberate from your belly and directly experience how you cast off your burden. Do this as many times as you need to. If your thoughts are active, allow them to be there. Simply observe them intently as they pass through. Feel yourself relax, allowing any tight muscles to simply let go. Although completely relaxed, stay alert and attentive, noticing any physical sensations as well as thoughts going through the mind,...... noticing all sensations and thoughts, but not getting hooked on them. Focus now, on the subject you wish to explore more deeply:

The Principle of Enlightenment/Step 2

To openly receive what you need, is as important as asking for it. Due to ingrained conditioning, that you "are not good enough", that deep down "you are unworthy", very often we are just not able to receive our blessings, the good things that do come our way and even less, the goodness that resides in our own Heart.

For everyone, including yourself, even if you have not been graced with the best of luck, life offers countless treasures. We often fail to notice them, however, because the best ones are within us. If we will only slow down and tune in, inside us is a vast reservoir of Grace, just waiting to be tapped. Instead of allowing ourselves to acknowledge these blessings, we continue to struggle and strive, searching outside of ourselves for an elusive mirage, which will disappear as soon as the body is no longer with us. We deplete our Life Force in the process - when all we really have to do, is simply receive.

Receiving our blessings seems to be the greatest challenge for most of us, yet it is the essential conclusion and cap stone to the process of self-healing. When we finally, with much initial reluctance, bring ourselves to ask for what we need, there is one more step to take, and that is to receive what we need. We can open ourselves and foster the hidden strength in vulnerability, which allows us to receive.

Most humans feel shy about coming out and asking for true prosperity and sovereignty in their lives. To put energy behind their efforts to bring about this wish is an even greater challenge. Some finally do, but even fewer are able to stay openhearted enough to fully receive this prosperity to the point of enjoying it, spreading it and sharing it intelligently. Many people claim that they want to be physically healthy and emotionally balanced, but don't really ask for it from the bottom of their Heart. Most are unconsciously attached to their suffering because it is familiar and often provides secondary benefits (such as getting to play the martyr). Some finally do ask, but even fewer receive the full benefit of the treasures that a human existence has to offer. Most humans feel terribly inhibited to ask for Love, and for those who do, even fewer are willing to open themselves and receive the unconditional Love that is always there for the taking.

One could go on with all the reasons for this self-defeating behavior. However, all the reasons in the world won't change a thing. What is important, is to sit quietly with yourself for a moment, exploring the possibility to receive the blessings that are meant for you.

Sitting quietly, yet attentively, put your left hand on your heart and your right hand on top of it. Feel your heartbeat, however faint it may be. Then close your eyes and smile. Let this smile become radiant and strong, and then draw it into your heart. Now, let your heart smile, sending out beams of contentment. These rays of contentment open the heart even further so that it can now receive the countless blessings that are meant for you, as a rose receives the morning sun. Remember: whatever blessings you may receive in your life, are just a reflection and refraction of the boundless blessings that resides in your Heart of hearts.

The Principle of Enlightenment/Step 3

Now, read the following statement out loud three consecutive times, giving a voice to your heart and true nature, strong and filled with the conviction of what is so:

For the sake of my well-being and that of my loved ones
And all of Creation,

From now until Awareness is recognized as all-pervasive,
I allow myself to receive what I truly need:
To receive comfort;
To receive the peace that I AM;
To receive what makes me healthy and strong;
To receive the gift of freedom from inside;
To receive the wisdom of my direct insights;
To receive the Love that is embedded in every cell of
my body
And in every particle of this vast Creation.

I give myself permission to receive all that is wholesome.

I let it spring forth from the depths of my liberated
Heart.

I receive it reflected in my world and in the people that I
meet.

Henceforth, in this very moment, I receive what
I truly need.

May the power and liberation inherent in this
all-embracing
Act of receiving the original blessing of Creation
prevail,

Thus bestowing happiness, and health and true
equanimity and relieving suffering everywhere.

The Principle of Enlightenment/Step 4

Sit quietly for a few moments and absorb the impact of your exploration as well as the words that you have just read out loud three times. Feel your own truth radiating throughout, gently, patiently and gradually repatterning your body/mind into a matrix of health and wholesomeness.

The Principle of Enlightenment/Step 5

Finally take five to ten minutes to write your observations for the day in the special diary that you have acquired for the 40-Day Program to Absolute Wellness.

Days 37-40

To conclude the program, four days of silent meditation and contemplation are required to help integrate the many energetic shifts that were stimulated by the process of deep self-exploration, both on a conscious and an unconscious level. This silent meditation and contemplation unfold in three distinct steps involving the awareness of body, breath and mind. From start to finish, the entire process through steps 1-3 should take you 30 minutes.

Step 1

Find a comfortable sitting posture, either in a chair or on the floor on a meditation mat and cushion, that allow you to sit upright without being rigid. Your spine is erect. Imagine that you are pulled slightly upward by an imaginary string attached to the top of your head so that your chin is slightly tucked in and the back of your neck automatically opens. Your breath flows naturally and you do not need to control it or try to slow it down.

Use your awareness to explore. Feel into the different areas of the body. First feel into the area around the eyes and notice if there is any feeling of strain or subtle tension. Spend a few moments and let your awareness fully feel into the area around the eyes. From the eyes, let your awareness shift to the area around and inside your ears, exploring them in the same fashion, always taking note of whatever sensations you find, feeling them fully. From the ears your awareness now moves down to your mouth. Feel into your mouth and around your mouth, as well as into your jaws, taking note of any sensations or any sense of excess tension, allowing these feelings to expand.

Continue in the same fashion, letting awareness explore and touch first the front of your body all the way down into the groin, feeling into each area and establishing how it feels. Always lingering however long it takes, until there is a sense of awareness actually penetrating and suffusing the area with its presence. Once you have completed the front of your body, feel all along your spine from the top of your head down into the tailbone. When your exploration reaches the level of your shoulders, also feel into both arms and hands.

After that, spend some time feeling into the area between the shoulder blades and behind the heart. Once you have felt all the way into the small of the back, continue your exploration into the entire pelvic area and into both legs and feet, until the entire body seems to glow with the presence of awareness.

Step 2

In this step, you switch your focus from bodily sensations to the breath and to the incessant interplay between body and breath. Start out by continuing to sit comfortably upright, either in a chair or on the floor on your meditation mat and cushion. Make sure that your spine is erect, yet not rigid. Just feel into your back and let your body find a natural alignment for your spine that has a flowing quality, effortless and graceful.

Then feel into your mouth and let it be slightly open so that the tip of the tongue touches the palate. Let your breath flow evenly and very gently through both nose and mouth simultaneously. You are breathing in through both nose and mouth, and you are breathing out through both nose and mouth, evenly and gently. Yet this process of breathing happens very naturally, and your awareness does not keep a tight grip on it. Rather it flows with it. It relaxes with the breathing and into the breathing so that, eventually, it becomes a very soft and gentle presence – as soft and gentle as your breathing.

Feel how subtly invigorating and energizing this gentle breathing is, and let your awareness completely merge with your breath. Now let the unified presence of awareness and soft breathing touch any physical sensation that occurs. For example, let it touch a muscle tension and observe what happens to the tension. Let it touch whatever occurs: a sensation, a feeling, a memory, a daydream, a thought.

Step 3

Continue to explore this unified presence of awareness and breathing, but now start to gently focus more on the thoughts that may arise, instead of on the feelings and sensations. Especially, let any insights and experiences that you may remember from your 36 days of self-exploration be touched by this soft awareness and breathing. Without trying to do anything in particular, observe if they naturally become more expansive, when touched by your gentle and light breathing together with your gentle and soft awareness.

The trick is to not try to add anything or make anything bigger. You also no longer need to intentionally expand thoughts, sensation or emotions. Simply let the thoughts and memories be touched by the breath that is also awareness, always allowing them to be there. In this way they expand of their own accord. They become even lighter, more transparent, more translucent. They adopt a space-like quality, which in turn can again be touched by the unified presence of your soft breathing and awareness.

Let this process continue and unfold until there is a sense of completion. Until you feel nourished, invigorated and healed by this new way of perceiving, which allows everything to be there, yet completely open and transparent.

Congratulations!

You have successfully completed 40 days of self-inquiry. Whether you realize it or not, these 40 days of uninterrupted practice have set in motion a shift in your awareness. A seed has been planted and nurtured, which will help you to perceive your life in a new way. If you have participated fully, especially in the expansion exercises, you will notice less resistance to unpleasant circumstances. The old issues and people that always seemed to "push your buttons" will evoke little or no emotional charge. This is because you have learned to feel whatever comes up, without resistance. That which still evokes resistance, may give you a little charge, but as you simply focus on it, observing it with your full attention, fully embracing the resistance, the charge dissipates.

Although it may not seem so, what you have completed is actually a very great accomplishment, as few people have the desire, let alone manage to take the time off for themselves, to nourish the Grace of clear perception. Sadly this is much to their own detriment.

In this day and age, our awareness is constantly pulled away from its own natural center, which leads to an unbalanced and eventually unhappy life. The only remedy for this trend toward distracting and scattering the mind until our senses are numbed out and our Life Force is spent on trivial and inconsequential pursuits, is to focus on what is happening in the moment.

There is great power and wisdom in every moment (which we soon discover is only one eternal moment) and in every event that unfolds in our lives, as it is a reflection of the innate power and wisdom inherent in Consciousness. However, this power and wisdom goes unnoticed when we don't allow ourselves to feel, when we instead opt only for the "figuring out" mode of doing things. When we feel the moment, we don't even have to seize it, because we are not separate from it.

There is great power and wisdom in feeling every moment of your life. In fact, it is the only way to empower yourself and to realize who you truly are. Only through awareness can you uncover the absolute confidence residing in Self. Only through awareness can you be free from outside manipulation. Awareness is the key for balance, health and happiness.

Do not be concerned if you seem to notice more acutely all the silly and foolish patterns you engage in. The truth is, you have always engaged in them, you simply didn't notice them in the same way you do now. The secret is not to judge yourself or others for the patterns that stand out so vividly now. Simply embrace them, love them, knowing they are all on automatic due to your and everyone else's conditioning. Just notice that as Awareness ItSelf, You Are Free already. Body/mind is just doing its thing. The paradox is, now that you notice this, you will begin to exercise real choice, when you catch yourself in the middle of the next pattern and decide to disengage from it.

Cultivating a liberating view and experience, can be a time consuming affair. But if you pay attention, it is exhilarating every step of the way. Instead of focusing on what didn't happen for you, focus on the many little shifts and changes that did in fact happen, and build on those.

From now on, just make it a habit to feel yourself, and to feel your life. And through this direct experience of your own life, many good things will come to pass. Allow them to happen and receive them with open arms, as you uncover more and more of the natural wisdom and compassion, which are your birthright as a human being.

Congratulations for being so humble and so strong.

Congratulations for being real with yourself and the world.

Chapter 12

We Can Help Each Other!

Self-Healing & the 40-Day Program
As a Tool for Support Groups

Come sit with me on this boulder. We will take turns boring the auger into stone. It is not such hard work when more than one is working. We will tell each other stories. We will help each other to do the task of our lives. We will wear away this stone without violence... We will talk to the granite. We will not give up. We will be like drops of water falling on a stone.

— *Christina Baldwin*

Together, the 9 Principles and the 40-Day Program to Absolute Wellness provide a wonderful tool to be shared with others. They can serve as pointers for a group of like-spirited people to explore and slowly accommodate a radical change in their basic outlook. If we make it a habit to apply them in our everyday existence, they will truly transform the values we live by, as when we heal ourselves, we truly heal our world. When we learn to co-exist within ourselves with all of our little habits, fears, hang-ups, as well as with our bliss, intuitive knowledge, vastness, and

Truth, we automatically learn to co-exist with others who share that same make-up of appearing to be simultaneously limited and limitless.

When we become partners with our imbalances and ailments, as well as with our resources and strengths, we become fit for a partnership society. We become empowered to live in harmony with our Earth family and with the even larger family of the countless beings that populate the cosmos. When as a precious human being, you are really at peace and live from the vastness of your own nature, Gods and demons alike will come to visit you, to partake of this Peace, to feel the Silence and Compassion of the true nature of an Integral Being. A first step in this direction can be to practice the 40-Day program together with others in a support group, dedicated to the same goal of individual and communal health and sanity.

To help the participant in this program develop self-discipline, we have so far addressed the issue of self-healing from the perspective of a path that every person has to follow individually. This is a valid approach to begin with, because for self-healing to happen we need to develop discipline, and first and foremost, we need to discipline ourselves. We also must go through our own unique healing process. No one can do it for us. Another person cannot notice what is troubling us with the same clarity that we can. No one else can feel and process our feelings for us, as no one has the same memories, dreams and recurrent thought patterns. Thus, no one can take action on our behalf, in a way that will allow us to reap the full benefits.

We can only live our own life and learn from its experiences (which is precisely why we are here on this Earth). No one else can live through our lessons or learn from them, in the way that we can. After all, they are our lessons. Each person has their own.

But does this mean that we have to remain isolated? Does the fact that we have to live our own life and learn our own lessons mean that there are no others sharing their lives with us? There are now around 7 billion people on this planet. We are one big community, one gigantic extended Earth family. And we all share the same dreams of health, happiness, peace and prosperity, irrespective of gender, race and religion.

That we are for the most part an unhappy family, and that our dreams are often disrupted, is another story. The fact remains that we are in this together. If we are ever going to pull ourselves out of the mess that we are in, we will have to do it together – both alone and together. Meaning, that each and every human being has to go through their own process. However we can share our individual processes with each other. Sharing these processes with each other is an expression of true compassion.

The reasons for our unhappiness as a planetary family are the same as those which make our individual life miserable: alienation, a festering sense of separation, insensitivity, unprocessed traumas and tons of denial. Or in more old-fashioned terms: Ignorance, greed and aversion - ignorance as to who we truly are, greed for what we believe to be desirable and is not yet acquired by us, and aversion toward what we resent and which is only too much a part of us. This is why self-exploration is so crucial not only for our own life but also for the life of the planet.

We are like a cell in the limitless and timeless vastness that we call universe. More specifically, we are a cell in this space-time phenomena, called "Planet Earth". Much in the same way as each cell in our own body is in instantaneous communication and has a direct link with all the other cells of our body, we as cells of the Earth are also in constant communication (albeit only on a subconscious level) with all the other cells of the Earth; i.e.: all living and inert matter. If we are effected by imbalance and disease, all the other cells feel the repercussions, although they most likely will not notice it, as the effect is infinitesimally small. Yet it exists, and it is accumulative. The more cells of the body that are sick, the more the entire body becomes sick. The more unhealthy and unbalanced people that walk the Earth, the more unhealthy and unbalanced the Earth will be. So, if we heal ourselves, we do indeed contribute to the healing of all other beings, as well as to the balance of the planet as a whole.

It is therefore important that we share our self-exploration with others so that we can nurture and support one another along the way. When we do this, we help each other to uphold our discipline and mirror each other's progress. We also immediately discover that we are not alone with our particular challenges but that many others face tasks at least as formidable as ours. Sharing with others gives us a more realistic perspective on our own predicament and serves to deflate any inappropriate or overblown self-pity.

The 40-Day Program to Self-Healing is an ideal medium for such sharing. It really helps to experience and discuss your results in a small or even larger group, to gain more clarity on your own process. If you feel drawn to, you can even assemble daily (if logistically possible) to practice together.

The 40-Day Program in an Established Support Group

If you feel inspired to use this book in a support group that already has been established, you will most likely have your own protocol and a fairly clear idea on how to incorporate and utilize the 40-Day Program within the existing framework. In that case, go right ahead.

Familiarize yourself thoroughly with the material, and if you are leading a group, follow the program for 40 consecutive days, before presenting it to others. When you finally introduce it to your group, remain true to the spirit of both the program and the book, which is one of unrestrained and unlimited self-exploration, conducted and based on the direct knowledge of non-duality. There is no absolute separation, only an illusion of separation between you and the world and you and your experiences. There are also no taboo zones, and no areas that cannot or should not be investigated. Everything is open for inquiry, and your direct intuitions and feelings are the gateway through which this enquiry proceeds.

If you come together without a leader in a support group that is organized as a circle of equals, every member of the group should first read the material at home. There needs to be enough time to reflect on it sufficiently, and then you must come to a unanimous decision, if you should or should not adopt this process for the circle. The decision needs to be unanimous because the process goes very deep, and this kind of depth can only manifest, when there is the willingness to go there and the acceptance to receive. No one can be forced to do the 40-Day Program against his or her will. It is impossible. It would also violate the spirit of open self-inquiry. Therefore, a majority decision is just not good enough. Consensus is what is needed.

When you have come to a decision, follow the program to the letter. Don't add anything, don't leave anything out, and don't change anything. If you compromise the program in any fashion, you compromise its value. The program can only produce the intended results of total Self-acceptance in the deepest sense of the word when you honor its form, as its particular form is the matrix that allows for a limitless variety of experiences.

The 40-Day Program in a New Support Group to Be Specifically Created for Its Exploration and Sharing

After reading the book and reflecting on its basic themes, you may feel inspired to form your own circle or support group. In this case, there are a few points to consider, especially if you have no experience with group processes. However, even if you are a complete newcomer, remember that there are no insurmountable obstacles ever, only challenges.

A support group doesn't have to be huge. Two people coming together with the motivation to explore and to share are as perfect a size for a support group as a larger gathering. A sacred circle of two is definitely an option, as you don't have to think big to make this one work. To make this work, you only need dedication and honesty. Dedication to go through the entire process and fully involve yourself, and honesty in the sense that you stop denying your feelings, and that you share your experiences honestly, the way you experienced them, without adding and without subtracting.

To set up a support group to study the 40-Day Program, you will have to state your intentions and invite people into the circle. You'll need to explain what you are up to. For example: "I would like us (meaning you plus the people you invite) to come together in an opening circle to discuss practicing the 40-Day Program of Self-Healing individually, and then have weekly group meetings to share our experiences. I want a commitment from each participant that the group will stay together for the entire process and have monthly follow-up meetings for another three months to share the mid-term repercussions of the process."

Naturally, you can also propose that the practices be done in daily group meetings, if such is logistically feasible. This will be a particularly powerful encounter for the entire group, as you will reinforce each other's energies. Sitting together in silence in focused self-inquiry expanding certain feelings, and then chanting out loud the life affirming verses that follow, creates a potent outer sacred space that will deeply nourish your inner sacred space. If you have a chance to practice together in this way, we strongly suggest that you avail yourself of it. You will be amazed by what it can do for each and every member of the circle. Consequently, the sharing will also go deeper, and accommodate the spirit of vulnerability needed for sharing from the Heart, which fosters self-transcending honesty.

Some Healthy Guidelines for Working In a Support Group or Circle

Once a support group or circle has been formed, there are certain guidelines that can help sustain it in a fruitful way for its duration. These need to be respected. If they are not, the benefits will be severely compromised, and unhealthy emotional reactions will most likely flare up and destroy the work that has been done or could have been done.

1. EQUALITY: Guideline number one is to respect the spirit of equality, the fact that each participant is as valuable to the group or circle as any other is. That is why, for example, the American *Declaration of Independence* proclaims the self-evident truth that "all men are created equal". Equality does not mean that we are all the same, but that we are of the same value. Equal value leaves much room for diversity, and does not propose a lack of difference. To honor diversity by honoring essential equality is a prerequisite for your support group or circle to function successfully. Although such mention may sound unnecessary because everyone seemingly understands this, we nevertheless have to bring it up, simply because this truth is only superficially adopted, and not integrated into the way we live our everyday lives. No matter which place on the planet we call home, we all have been brought up in hierarchical structures that discourage or outright deny equality. In the family, in our education, and at work, everywhere we are forced to operate and express ourselves in the framework of the pyramid structure. Pyramid structure means that there are only a chosen few at the top who hold all the information and all the power in their hands. Then, as you go down the pyramid level by level, knowledge and power also go down, until you reach the bottom where there are hardly any vestiges of knowledge and power left. We may not notice it and we may not like it, but we are all psychologically and emotionally altered and damaged by this hierarchical approach, inherent in the pyramid power structure of our homes, businesses and government institutions. It will therefore be difficult for us to leave our conditioning at the door, when we enter the sacred circle of the group. This is why we need to consciously evoke the spirit of equality, as in the circle, we are all equally part of the rim, whereas the center is the sacred and empty space, whence our inquiry unfolds. We need to open our hearts to the fact that in the sacred circle, we all equally share one Heart, yet use our different voices to express it in many different ways.

2. RESPONSIBILITY: The change from a hierarchical structure to a structure based on essential equality necessitates a change in the way responsibility is shared. In the pyramid structure all responsibilities are delegated from the top down, whereas all rights remain the prerogative of the "chosen few" that are placed "high up". The further down you go in the pyramid, the longer grows the list of responsibilities and obligations that need to be fulfilled, the further up you climb the more privileges you believe you are destined to enjoy. Leadership stays ensconced at the top either with one person, or with selected individuals. Such hierarchical thinking does not apply in the circle. In the support group or circle, rights and responsibilities are equally shared, which should involve rotating leadership. In other words, when you meet as a group let someone else lead the group every time you get together.

3. SPIRITUALITY: The pyramid is a power· structure, designed to perpetuate Samsara. It may superficially proclaim to have spiritual goals, yet is actually solely interested in worldly power and privilege. Religions are pyramid structures. Spirituality presents itself in the form of a circle and feels motivated to transcend Samsara. Pyramid and circle are incompatible. Pyramid power has a vested interest in destroying the circle, as it despises equality. The circle has a selfless motivation for the good of all concerned, to slowly permeate and change the pyramid from within, to soften it up and transform it. The pyramid forces the people entrapped in its multileveled structure to deny their own nature, and to live a lie. The circle acknowledges that in each and everyone there is truth, and that this truth has the right to express itself as long as it does not infringe upon another. The pyramid demands adherence to the letter of the law. The circle evokes tolerance and relies on the spirit of Universal Law. Therefore, when we come together as a support group or in a circle to practice the 40-Day Program, we need to understand and respect the deeply spiritual nature of our gathering. If we do, we shall meet in truth, which in Sanskrit is called "Satsang" – meeting in the Truth That Is.

There are many fine points that need to be taken into account, most of which you will intuitively grasp anyway. However, if you wish to study the subject of meeting in groups among equals any further, we suggest you read Christina Baldwin's wonderful book: *Calling the Circle – The First and Future Culture*. It will give you many additional handy hints about coming together as a group.

Chapter 13

The 9 Principles of Self-Healing

1

The Principle of Self Respect

When we have self respect, we don't tolerate being rushed. Even when under pressure we manage to remain deliberate. We savor each moment and come to our own conclusions when and how it feels right for us. We honor the world by truly perceiving it. We honor ourselves by allowing the space and time we need, in all of our endeavors. In this way, every moment of our life is an invitation for self-discovery and an opportunity for the recognition of Truth.

2

The Principle of Awareness

When in harmony with the natural flow of awareness, we notice every major and minor aspect in the complex tapestry of our existence. We drop the fetters of unconscious behavior and slowly disengage from

*ignorance. We enter the path of a true human being.
With every instance of conscious awareness, we water
the roots of the tree of Life and grow in Freedom.*

3 ⌒

The Principle of Letting Go

*By diving into our feelings and exploring them from
the inside out, we let go of unhealthy clinging. The
power that our unconscious and unacknowledged
feelings once had over us, from this moment onward,
flows through us. The congealed power that kept us
stuck and in bondage is now liberated to fuel our
creativity. Feeling our feelings fully and letting them
go of their own accord, we increase our awareness of
the hidden beauty within all appearances. As we
embrace our feelings, we are rejuvenated, becoming
more flexible and responsive.*

4 ⌒

The Principle of Courage

*We are conditioned to relegate what we don't know
into the shadowy recesses of the mind. What lurks in
the shadows, we usually fear. By summoning courage
we are able to face the shadows that are only the
projections of our fear. The greatest fear we have is
that of death. Death can be physical, as in the body
dying. Death can be symbolic, as in the ego being
exposed as the illusion it is. By facing our greatest fear*

with courage, it becomes our fiercest ally and protector, similar to the darkest shadow that eventually reveals its innate light.

5 ⌐

The Principle of Compassion

To be free is to let go of the conditioning of the past, as well as any hope for the future. As long as we can't forgive what has happened in the past we remain fettered. To forgive therefore, is a gesture of true compassion. It frees us from the bondage of past history. It severs the rope with which our grudges have tied others to our destiny, thereby releasing our burdens us as well as their. When unconditional, true compassion can reach out in complete openness as if with a thousand seeing hands.

6 ⌐

The Principle of Responsibility

This principle is called the Principle of Empowerment, because taking on and fulfilling responsibility is the only truly empowering and satisfying experience for a human being. When we start taking responsibility, we also start to master life and cease being a victim, tossed around by circumstance. Responsibility culminates in the experience that as Consciousness, we are the creator of our entire life. As the creator we can never be powerless victims. Once we experience this indivisible Truth, we are indeed home free.

7

The Principle of Love

Love is caring. Love is tenderness. Love is also passionate. When we embrace our troubles tenderly like a mother caring for her child, our troubles cease to be our enemies. They become like our children whose misbehavior we accept without judgment; whom we give space to expand and grow, until their resistance simply dissipates. With enough practice and awareness, we can learn how to dance the dance of enlightenment with passionate self-abandon, even in the greatest adversity. Through the embrace of such passionate Love, everything is released.

8

The Principle of Devotion

Our true needs are our calling in life. They have drawn us here into this existence. The way to fulfill them is to honor them. When we discover what we truly need and ask for it, our life's purpose can be fulfilled. Also, when we have the courage to ask, our heart opens and allows us to receive our good. The key element here, is devotion. Whims and fantasies never inspire devotion. Only our heartfelt need can. However, to uncover our

genuine need, we also have to learn how to fulfill our
little needs. If fulfilled wisely, they will lead us to the
devotion inherent in heartfelt need.

9 ᐟ

The Principle of Enlightenment

As much as enlightenment is not a goal, but one
continuous reality, health and balance are our natural
state, not something we need to strive for. Only when
we appear to have strayed from our nature, do we
appear to need to strive to regain our health and
balance. Enlightenment permeates all of existence. It
is ever present. We cannot find it outside of ourselves
or in an imaginary future because it is already here. It
is simply a matter of receiving It, through surrender
to That, which we truly Are. In the same way, on the
deepest level, we cannot even seek and find health and
balance, as they are already given. It is through
openness and receptivity, that our natural state of
balance is realized. This is basic sanity and the end of
all strife.

Bibliography

Airola, Paavo: *Are You Confused? – The Authoritative Answer to Controversial Questions*, Phoenix, 1971, Health Plus Publishers

Airola, Paavo: *Every Woman's Book – Dr. Airola's Practical Guide to Holistic Health*, Phoenix, 1979, Health Plus Publishers

Baldwin, Christina: *Calling the Circle, The First and Future Culture*, Newberg, 1994, Swan Raven

Blofeld, John: *I Ching – The Book of Change*, New York, 1991, Arkana

Brecher, Harold & Arline: *Forty Something Forever – A Consumer's Guide to Chelation Therapy*, Herndon, 1992, Health Savers Press

Chopra, Deepak: *The Seven Spiritual Laws of Success – A Practical Guide to the Fulfillment of Your Dreams*, San Rafael, 1994 Amber-Allen Publishing & New World Library

Dalai Lama: *The Path to Tranquility - Daily Meditations*, New Delhi, 1998, Penguin India

Das, Surya Lama: *Awakening to the Sacred – Creating a Spiritual Life From Scratch*, New York, 1999, Broadway Books

Dossey, Larry: *Space, Time & Medicine*, Boulder & London, 1982, Shambhala Publications

Gerson, Max: *A Cancer Therapy – Results of 50 Cases; A Summary of 30 Years of Clinical Experimentation*, Bonita, 1986, Gerson Institute

Horan, Paula: *Abundance through Reiki - Universal Life Force Energy as Expression of the Truth That You Are, with the 42-Day Program to   Absolute Fulfillment*, Twin Lakes, 1995, Lotus Light

Jampolsky, Gerald: *Love Is Letting Go of Fear*, Berkeley, 1979, Celestial Arts

Matthiessen, Peter: *Nine-Headed Dragon River, Zen Journals 1969 – 1982*, Boston, 1985, Shambhala Publications

McCabe, Ed: *O₂xygen Therapies, A New Way of Approaching Disease*, Morrisville, 1988, Energy Publications

Mithal, C.P.: *Miracles of Urine Therapy*, New Delhi, Pankaj Books

Ni, Hua Ching: *Hua Hu Ching, The Later Teachings of Lao-Tzu*, Boston & London, 1995, Shambhala Publications

Ni, Hua Ching: *I Ching – The Book of Changes and the Unchanging Truth*, Santa Monica, 1990, Seven Star Communications Group

Page, Linda: *Healthy Healing Guide to Cancer*, Carmel Valley, 1997, Healthy Healing Publications

Poonja, H.W.L.: *The Truth Is*, New Delhi, 2001, Full Circle Publishing

Rappoport, Jon: *Health Freedom Wins – The Death Monopoly Loses*, a Report

Samson, G.B.: *Japan - A Short Cultural History*, New York, 1962, Appelton-Century Crofts

Taylor, Renee: *Hunza Health Secrets for Long Life and Happiness*, New Canaan, 1978, Keats Health Book

Trungpa, Chögyam: *Crazy Wisdom*, Boston & London, 1991, Shambhala Publications

Tulku, Tarthang: *Gesture of Balance – A Guide to Awareness, Self-Healing and Meditation*, Berkeley, 1977, Dharma Publishing

Tulku, Tarthang: *Knowledge of Freedom – Time to Change*, Berkeley, 1984, Dharma Publishing

Resources

At different places in the book, references to complementary approaches to different health problems are made. All of these approaches are available and accessible in most countries, although it may take some dedicated effort to trace down practitioners. If you are interested in additional information, contact the web-site: www.paulahoran.com where you will find a number of references. You can also leave a message with a specific question, and someone will get back to you within 3 to 4 weeks.

In case you wish to share your experiences with the book and the program with others, you may do so through the web-site: www.paulahoran.com. Once a year, a circle will be organized where you can sign up to do the 40-Day Program together with others and share your insights and experiences on a regular basis. A message board will be set up to stay in touch with other practitioners.

About the Authors

PAULA HORAN is a psychologist, experienced in a wide variety of therapeutic approaches. She is also a respected leader in the Reiki community and best-selling author of six previous books, some of which were translated into 15 languages. From 1992 to 1997, she spent much of her time with her master Shri H.W.L. Poonja (also affectionately known as Papaji), a self-realised being who left his body in September 1997. Inspired by his message of non-duality, she shifted her focus from self-improvement to self-inquiry. At present, she divides her time between India and Nepal. While in India, she focuses mostly on research and writing. In Nepal, she is undergoing a regular course of training with two accomplished Tibetan yogis of the Nyingma lineage.

NARAYAN CHÖYIN DORJE has been a book translator and free-lance editor for most of his professional life. He has also been a student and practitioner of Tibetan and Taoist yoga for over 20 years and studied with some of the leading teachers of our time. *The 9 Principles of Self-Healing* is the first book where he is acknowledged as co-author. He chose to combine the names given to him by Papaji and his present Tibetan teacher into a pen name, as he feels that these names speak more to his essence than the name he received at birth. He also feels motivated to demonstrate his gratitude to his teachers to whom he knows he owes so much. Although experienced in the field of self-help books, his true passion is the poetry of the Spirit. He lives together with Paula in South India and Nepal and is presently working on several more writing projects, as well as on ongoing spiritual training. He leads *Nadi Prana Release* retreats upon request, and co-teaches *Medicine Dharma Reiki* and the *Core Empowerment Training* together with Paula.

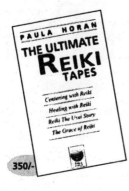

Join the

WORLD WISDOM BOOK CLUB

Get the best of world literature in the comfort of your home at fabulous discounts!

Benefits of the Book Club

Wherever in the world you are, you can receive the best of books at your doorstep.

- Receive FABULOUS DISCOUNTS by mail or at the **FULL CIRCLE** Bookstore in Delhi.

- Receive Exclusive Invitations to attend events being organized by **FULL CIRCLE**.

- Receive a FREE copy of the club newsletter — The World Wisdom Review — every month.

- Get UP TO 25% OFF.

Join Now!

It's simple. Just fill in the coupon overleaf and mail it to us at the address below:

FULL CIRCLE
J-40, Jorbagh Lane, New Delhi 110003
Tel: 24620063, 55654197 • Fax: 24645795 • www.atfullcircle.com

FULL CIRCLE

FULL CIRCLE publishes books on inspirational subjects, religion, philosophy, and natural health. The objective is to help make an attitudinal shift towards a more peaceful, loving, non-combative, non-threatening, compassionate and healing world.

FULL CIRCLE continues its commitment towards creating a peaceful and harmonious world and towards rekindling the joyous, divine nature of the human spirit.

Our fine books are available at all leading bookstores across the country.

FULL CIRCLE *PUBLISHING*

Editorial Office
J-40, Jorbagh Lane, New Delhi-110003
Tel: 24620063, 55654197, 30973793 • Fax: 24645795
E-mail: fullcircle@vsnl.com / gbp@del2.vsnl.net.in
website: www.atfullcircle.com

Bookstores
5B, Khan Market, New Delhi-110003
Tel: 24655641, 24655642
N-8, Greater Kailash Part I Market, New Delhi-110048
Tel: 26475641-42

Warehouse & Sales Office
B-13, Sector-81, Phase-II, NOIDA (UP) - 201305
Tel: 55654198, 0120-3093992